FIRE IN THE BELLY

How to write your novel with Purpose and Passion

by

Thornton Sully

FIRE IN THE BELLY

How to write your novel with Purpose and Passion

by

Thornton Sully

A Word with You Press

Editors and Advocates for Fine Stories in the Digital Age

with offices and affiliates in the USA, the UK, Germany, Poland, and the Czech Republic

www.awordwithyoupress.com

also by Thornton Sully

> *The Boy with a Torn Hat*
> *Almost Avalon*
> *Courtesans of God* (summer, 2021)

Anthologies:

> *The Coffeeshop Chronicles: Oh, the Places I have Bean!*
> *Kid Expressions 2012*
> *Inside the Lines—Outside the Box*
> *5×5: Keeping the Dream Aloft*

"The most powerful weapon on earth is a spirit on fire."

Ferdinand Foch,
prevailing French general, WWI

www.awordwithyoupress.com

Sully, Thornton
Fire in the Belly:
How to write your novel with Purpose and Passion

ISBN-13: 978-1-7365480-0-4

Fire in the Belly is published by:
A Word with You Press

For information please direct emails to:
thorn@awordwithyoupress.com or visit our website:
www.awordwithyoupress.com

Book cover and interior designed by A Word with You Press
Front cover photos: Shutterstock.com, Pexels / Pixabay
Back cover photo: Public Co / Pixabay

First Edition, March, 2021

Printed in the United States of America

10 9 8 7 6 5 4 3 2 1   21 22 23 24 25 26 27 28 29 30

Dedication

For Eszter, who helps me tell *my* story, unedited

As the program manager of Pen in the Classroom, it is my pleasure to endorse Thornton Sully as a capable and inspiring creative writing instructor. His engaging teaching style and unique lesson plans helped draw stories out of our students and convinced them that they were talented, innovative storytellers. Thorn's students produced an anthology of truly compelling stories. I am happy to endorse any endeavor that Thorn germinates to help people discover their unique, creative voices and provide them with the tools they need to exercise their freedom of expression. I wish Thorn the very best of luck.

Heather Simons
Project manager,
PEN in the Classroom
PEN Center USA, Beverly Hills, Ca
www.penusa.org

Hey Thorn,

Sometimes, you don't know you're in a fog until the sun shines through. Thank you for sending me Fire in the Belly. It's perfect for a new writer like me. I'm trying to address many of the things I'm learning about: fewer-info dumps/fewer adverbs, adjs/Active vs. Passive voice /alliterations/sarcasm/ metaphor/simile, tightening, trimming, etc. etc. etc. I think my muse is you! Or your book!

Holly Butler, soon-to-be-published author of
Me, Myself, and Marilyn

The funny thing about working with Thorn is that I can't exactly say __what__ he does that helps me. Perhaps it's Thorn's practical wisdom on the art and craft of writing. I'm still not sure. All I know is I've become a better writer since working with Thorn.

Mark Cohen, author
Listening to the Echo

ACKNOWLEDGEMENTS

I am of a mind that the only people who read acknowledgements are those who think they *should* be acknowledged and want to certify they were not omitted. According to my friend and best-selling author Victor Villaseñor, a writer needs to be an "arrogant son-of-a-bitch," but I disagree, and this page is my best chance at humility.

Thank you, the hundreds of you I have published online and in print, and those who allowed me to provide comment and direction to your stories over the years. You caused me to be reflective, and I am grateful for the trust you placed in me. I did not teach you how to be better writers; you taught me how to be a better editor.

Thanks to all of you who allowed me to print your endorsements of my services listed in the tail/tale end of the book.

Since *A Word with You Press* was established in 2009, a steady stream of interns, volunteers, and contributing editors have helped me provide a forum for both fledgling and known writers to share their work online and in print, and several of these wonderful people have been with me for the past ten or twelve years: Stefani Allison, Derek Thompson, Ed Coonce, Tiffany Vakilian, Morgan Sully, Billy Holder, Kristy Webster, and, more recently, Ben Angel.

A special thanks to Arthur Salm, who 20 years ago as the editor of the Books Section gave me the privilege of writing reviews for the San Diego Union Tribune.

Every editor needs an editor. For this volume, I solicited and integrated the advice of publisher Barbara Villaseñor, Professor Ron McFarland, author Derek Thompson, and especially poet Lucien Zell, a fellow expat seduced by the beauty and splendor of living life in Prague and South Bohemia. Of our shared passion for the written word, Lucien reminds me "Fiction is our last chance at reality." Keep Lucien on your radar.

And lastly, firstly, and all points in between, thank you Eszter, my darling.

Table of Contents

FOREWORD

(or, perhaps more accurately, *Forward*)

I believe in the power and beauty of the written word. I believe that by writing your story skillfully, with honesty and artistry, you serve our basic human need to connect to one another. Using my experience and acquired knowledge to liberate and develop your innate potential as a writer is my pleasure and duty, my purpose and my passion, *my* fire in the belly.

There's work (play) to do. Let's not waste any time.

My very first piece of advice is that you take me up on the free offer you'll find in the first few pages. Simply email me with your answer to the quintessential question of why you write, and I'll respond *personally*—not a generic email—and review any three pages of work you'd like me to comment upon.

This book is arranged into 12 independent lessons, best read sequentially. Each lesson is followed by suggested assignments to help you gain altitude. My second piece of advice is that you really *do* the exercises, even if no one is watching.

You have two options to maximize your experience of *Fire in the Belly*.

One: Read the book, absorb what resonates and apply the insights at your discretion. You've paid for the book; we're good.

The second option is to enroll in the Interactive Course that supplements the text. This is for those of you determined to become published, sensing it can happen if you up your game.

Signing up for the course gets you up to 15 hours of one-on-one with an award-winning editor. Complete the assignments that follow each lesson and send them to me for comprehensive review and feedback. Upon graduating from the course, if you have submitted at least eight of the 12 exercises, *A Word with You Press* will issue you a Certificate of Completion. To those who demonstrate they've absorbed the principles taught in *Fire in the Belly* and applied them to their final composition, we'll mail a Certificate of Excellence.

The total fee for the course is deductible should you purchase a 20-hour block of time to apply to your work-in-progress or completed novel. Additionally, we'll discount by 10% the fees for all other services listed in the final pages of the book. Here's a link to payment details:

https://gumroad.com/l/IPaVR

Editors are the elder statesmen of the writing community, and we're eager to assist you to tell your story. Why? Because we know, as Maya Angelou has said:

"There is no greater agony than bearing an untold story inside you."
But you know that.
That's why you're here.
That's why *I'm* here.

Thornton Sully
Founder and Editor-in-Chief
A Word with You Press (est. 2009)

A Word with You Press

Editors and Advocates for Fine Stories in the Digital Age

with offices and affiliates in the USA, the UK, Germany, Poland, and the Czech Republic

www.awordwithyoupress.com

A Prologue

(Read the prologue. I put it here for a reason.)

WHY DO PEOPLE BOTHER TO WRITE AT ALL?

Think long and hard before you speculate. Reduce the enormity of the question by simply asking *yourself*, why do *you* write? Every *how-to* writing class you could ever take will result in a paint-by-numbers manuscript if you don't know *why* you're willing to walk on broken glass to free the words held hostage behind your computer screen. Without that certainty, you might fill in your canvas or fill up your word-count, but so what? When Beethoven was asked why he wrote music, he unflinchingly answered, "To change the world." This was not arrogance, but certainty.

Don't reserve a table for that first dinner date with your muse until you can declare *why* you are possessed to write. She's not into small talk and can spot a phony, but she'll feel your warmth if you have fire in the belly, and will sidle up to you, and willingly offer you inspiration and the words you'll need to seduce your readers if you're straight with her. Be worthy of her. Let her know *why* you write, and why you need her company. Do this, then *what* to write and *how* to write will fall into place like stardust.

Your first revelation by engaging in the muscle-building sessions presented here will be that you have *grossly* underestimated your abilities to write, and to write well. I will help you tap your potential; doing so is the nexus of all successful editor/writer partnerships. And here is a startling observation, hiding in plain sight: the same amount of effort invested into mediocre work can, if properly channeled from the start, result in brilliance. Trees are pruned as they grow.

Eric Blair (you might know him as George Orwell) had this to say:

> "Putting aside the need to earn a living, I think there are four great motives for writing, at any rate for writing prose. They exist in different degrees in every writer, and in any one writer the proportions will vary from time to time, according to the atmosphere in which he is living. They are:
>
> 1)   Sheer egoism. Desire to seem clever, to be talked about, to be remembered after death, to get your own back on grown-ups who

snubbed you in childhood, etc., etc. It is humbug to pretend this is not a motive, and a strong one. Writers share this characteristic with scientists, artists, politicians, lawyers, soldiers, successful businessmen – in short, with the whole top crust of humanity. The great mass of human beings are not acutely selfish. After the age of about thirty they abandon individual ambition—in many cases, indeed, they almost abandon the sense of being individuals at all—and live chiefly for others, or are simply smothered under drudgery. But there is also the minority of gifted, willful people who are determined to live their own lives to the end, and writers belong in this class. Serious writers, I should say, are on the whole more vain and self-centered than journalists, though less interested in money.

2) Aesthetic enthusiasm. Perception of beauty in the external world, or, on the other hand, in words and their right arrangement. Pleasure in the impact of one sound on another, in the firmness of good prose or the rhythm of a good story. Desire to share an experience which one feels is valuable and ought not to be missed. The aesthetic motive is very feeble in a lot of writers, but even a pamphleteer or writer of textbooks will have pet words and phrases which appeal to him for non-utilitarian reasons; or he may feel strongly about typography, width of margins, etc. Above the level of a railway guide, no book is quite free from aesthetic considerations.

3) Historical impulse. Desire to see things as they are, to find out true facts and store them up for the use of posterity.

4) Political purpose – using the word 'political' in the widest possible sense. Desire to push the world in a certain direction, to alter other people's idea of the kind of society that they should strive after. Once again, no book is genuinely free from political bias. The opinion that art should have nothing to do with politics is itself a political attitude."

———

What is it that writing does for you that no other pursuit can provide? Recently I published an anthology of stories by writers whose work I have posted sporadically online since establishing *A Word with You Press* over ten years ago. (*5×5: Keeping the Dream Aloft—Five authors, Five stories each*) I was impressed by the fact that they kept on writing, knowing that the chance of being published by a Random House was nil, as their work had no commercial viability (no zombies, boy-meets-boy scenarios, the usual suspects). I scattered throughout the anthology their own answers to *Why do you write?* Here's a sampling:

"I write because there are too many stories to tell, and not enough campfires to tell them around."

Ed Coonce

"I believe every writer is motivated by something uniquely their own. For me, writing is a way to overcome fear, loneliness and to connect with others. In my case, the fear of being judged, of being hurt, of being abandoned, must be met with absolute vulnerability. When others connect with that vulnerability, I know that the voice inside my head that tells me I'm alone, is a lie. My motivation has been to find a language for pain that doesn't leave the reader feeling hopeless. That doesn't leave *me* feeling hopeless. How can I express rejection, emotional wounds, and spiritual violation in an authentic, genuine manner, without being unnecessarily brutal to my readers? How do I find that middle place? In the end, I do not write about what I feel, I feel what I'm writing. A reader can sense the writer's voice if the writer is trying too hard, if they are only mimicking an emotion. The most powerful works in my opinion, are those that evoke empathy, that follow the natural curves of loss and redemption. I don't for a moment believe myself to be a great storyteller. Sometimes plot evades me. Some people will read my writing and ask, *What's the point?* That is what I most often expect. But what surprises me is when someone connects with the language and recognizes something deeply personal to them within my writing. It will always surprise me."

Kristy Webster

"... because I have a crush on words. I roll them on my tongue, admire their curves and angles, rub their long limbs with my intellect. Words make me fall in love (with people who send them to me, and with words themselves). It is a passionate, playful affair. Words are my paint box, the way I process beauty. Writing can turn any experience, however hard, into art. I grow emotionally by writing and reading, and often learn to forgive. Writing is redemptive."

Laura Elizabeth

"I write because I am a slave's dream come true, and in the Library of Babel, I cry out their echoes."

Tiffany Vakilian, Associate Editor
A Word with You Press, Vista, California
President, San Diego Book Awards

"I write to find beauty in places where people think that it could never exist. I write to challenge conventions. More often than not, however, I write to find beauty, especially in people."

Jon Tobias

"I've written for much of my post-second grade life, but now when I try to define the reason I write, I find the answer has been a moving target. I would have to admit that I write to remember, or perhaps, more honestly, I write to be remembered."

Ben Angel, Associate Editor,
A Word with You Press, Wroclaw, Poland

———

The great paradox is that introspective writers, by knowing only themselves in depth, can divine the aspirations, feelings, spirit and soul of an anonymous readership they will never meet. Does that describe you?

So ... why *do* you write? Ambiguity is not your friend.

You'll get the most out of these lessons if you know the answer with Beethovenian certainty and understand the difference between motivation and inspiration. *Motivation* is cerebral; it stirs your mind and the consequence could be a passing thunderstorm. A motivational reason/sentence why you write? "My grandparents died in Auschwitz, and I believe I can be of some influence on the present generation if I told their story." Same topic but energized by *inspiration* rather than simple *motivation*: "My grandparents took a shower at Auschwitz, and I'm the only one left to tell their story." *Inspiration* is what stirs within your breast, and the deluge could float the Ark. For a writer, inspiration must morph into compulsion bordering on obsession. A visceral, not a well-modulated cerebral experience.

If you want to become an editor, this book is indispensable. If you're curious what an editor is looking for in the stack of unsolicited manuscripts, the notorious slush pile, this book is also for you.

Or maybe you just want to write brilliantly?
That'll work.
Welcome!
Your table is waiting.

The New York Cafe in Budapest © Thornton Sully

A PROLOGUE

WORKOUT

Assignment: Write a long and short version of why you write. The short version should be a simple declarative statement. I write to:

The long version should be a mini-essay, about a page or at least a few paragraphs giving your statement historical context—your history. For example, if your declarative, motivational statement is "I write because I believe in social justice, and writing is my way of contributing to a more just society," then your essay should reveal some personal experience, the *inspiration*, that got you to that conclusion. "My father told me that when he was a child, he couldn't swim in the public pool because Mexican-Americans were not as clean as the white kids. He often recalled that indignity. As I saw him weaken with age, our roles reversed, and the loving man who had always protected me was now the one who needed protection, in this instance, from a life bludgeoned with the pain of a childhood that beat him up. I write because I loved my father." Or if you say something simple like "I write to be heard," trace it to how you felt as a child who stuttered or was habitually ignored at the dinner table. What was that experience like? What would you say to everyone who ignored you if they were listening now?

This assignment is an exercise in introspection. I am genuinely interested in what you have to say. Submit your answer, and regardless of whether or not you have signed up for the comprehensive Interactive Course, I will correspond personally (not a generic email) and waive my fee for professional feedback on any three pages of your work you care to send me.

 thorn@awordwithyoupress.com

I will respond with the same thoughtfulness you invest in your answer.

Piano Tuning:

THE PRELUDE TO PERFORMANCE

So, you want to be a writer?

Take your laptop to Starbucks and be seen composing your manuscript. Look concerned while concentrating on a stubborn passage. Look elated when you get it right. People will notice. Sip your latte; it's getting cold.

BUT! If you want to *write*, your focus is substance, not image, and the world is waiting to hear what you have to say, and somewhere in a galaxy, not so far, far away (that would be here) is an editor prepared to help you say it. In these lessons, I will help you say what's in your heart and on your mind persuasively, concisely, and with passion.

Writing a novel is the most noble of ambitions, and you are to be commended for launching yourself into it. A novel is "… the prose form by which an author thoroughly explores, by means of experimental selves (characters), some great theme of existence."—Milan Kundera, the still-living and actively writing author of *The Unbearable Lightness of Being*.

These lessons will shave months off your learning curve. I'll teach you the skills to *dis*passionately self-edit with confidence what you have so *passionately* written, before you turn your little darling over to a developmental editor (not your sister-in-law who teaches high school English). Let's storm the Bastille together, where the chapters of your manuscript huddle together, complaining about mold and longing for liberation.

Here's a sample of what we'll cover, or perhaps, more accurately, *un*cover:

Do you think that word choice simply implies the use of a thesaurus? What happens if you simply replace an indefinite article with a possessive pronoun? You can breezily multi-task while reading about *a* manuscript with an air of indifference, but it gets personal and compelling when I talk about *your* manuscript. Word choice has clout.

You might have taken it for *granite*, but your writer's block is soft as pumice, pulverized by the pounding of keys. Provisioning yourself with refreshing insights about attribution, literary devices, dialogue, and narrative will make you a better sorcerer to cast a spell on your readers, and, equally important, advance your career as a surgeon. Unnecessary words will tremble from fear of your terrible, swift scalpel, avoiding a wholesale liposuction of superfluous fat.

It's been my pleasure as an editor to discover stuff you probably haven't been exposed to, and the knowledge I've accumulated is what I'm offering you to assimilate, as I have to award-winning and best-selling authors.

I *can* help you, and your apprenticeship begins right now.

Ready?

Oh, wait! One more thing before we begin. I never lose sight of the fact that YOU are the world's leading authority on your own novel. Neither should you.

> "Don't bend; don't water it down; don't try to make it logical; don't edit your own soul according to the fashion. Rather, follow your most intense obsessions mercilessly."
>
> Franz Kafka

Kafka self-portraits

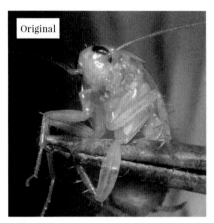

Your job as an editor is to amplify and clarify your client's vision, not alter it, unless you are specifically asked to make the work more marketable or appeal to a specific demographic.

Here's a flexersize.

Over the next few minutes, choose whether you will forever be intimidated by the staggering accomplishments of world-famous writers, or instead if you will take your place alongside them. Confidence is not arrogance. Choose between Wayne and Stuart. No middle ground. This flexercise will tilt the scale in favor of Stuart.

Mike Myers, a.k.a. Wayne
from *Wayne's World*

Al Franken, a.k.a. Stuart Smalley

Now, close your eyes. Neat trick if you are reading this rather than getting the video version. (Yes, I know I can't see you, but close your eyes anyway.) Imagine your favorite writer, the one you most admire, the one you are certain you could not emulate because they are so good, so god-like.

But let's break it down.

Begin to make a list of things you have in common with the writer with a Mt. Olympus zip code.

Are you the same age or generation? Same gender? Same gender orientation? Same nationality? Did you each fight in a war? Protest a war? Raised by an abusive parent, or are you each an abusive parent? Are you both recovering alcoholics or not-so-recovered? Did you both do jail time? Join the Peace Corps? Did you each lose a spouse to a car accident or terrible disease? Do you both ride horses? Play piano? Prefer dogs to cats? Vote Democratic? Speak with a lisp? Anorexic? Overweight? Hispanic? Anglo? Check "Other" when the census taker knocks on your door? Both ran in the Boston Marathon? Both introverted? Extraverted? Life of the party? Wallflower? Poor? Rich? Same world view? Are you both divorced/married the same number of times, are you both ... well ... you get the idea.

Make your own list of what you have in common with a writer who is just so-o-o-o good you can't possibly hope to be as good a writer as they are. But after you've completed your list, guess what? None of those similarities that you might start to think are important matter. All that matters is that one thing that never made your list:

At one time you and your favorite author, (drum roll) were both *illiterate*!

(Yeah. You can open your eyes.)

What this tells me, what this should tell *you*, is that writing is not a gift from God, bestowed upon the chosen few, but rather, writing is something that is *learned*. But why take my word for it?

> "It's none of their business you have to learn to write. Let them think you were born that way."

> Ernest Hemingway

If you can *feed* on feedback (*criticism* is a word already loaded with negative connotations—never use that word) and are willing to devote time, there is no reason you can't be as successful a writer as the one you need to knock off the pedestal, or at least, move over a bit to make room for you.

But what IS a successful writer?

You may have heard that much of the best work never gets published, or, at least, taken up by a major publisher. Based on the fact that some amazing manuscripts I've seen never owned real estate on the end caps of Barnes and Noble, I'd say it's true. We succumb to the tendency to measure success by how many books are sold. We are enculturated to quantify what success is, rather than qualify it. (Though of course, many books of high literary quality deservedly sell a kagillion copies. *Fifty Shades of Gray*?)

If you can adequately and accurately convey with words your thoughts and passions to another human being—your reader—you *are* a success. Worry (or not) about marketing after that or hire somebody to worry for you. Remember, only ONE agent needs to convince only ONE publisher that your book is worthy of investment.

And here is a thought: In the supply and demand economy, there is ALWAYS a demand for good writing, compelling stories well told. When a book has sucked you in between its covers, exhausting you with its passion and inspiration, and you've clawed through to the final page, never wanting it to end, how long is it before you crave another fix? That next book that readers hunger for may very well be the one lurking behind your computer screen.

Piano Tuning:

THE PRELUDE TO PERFORMANCE

WORKOUT

Assignment: Trace the origins of your desires to write. Pick any of these questions.

What was the first book you ever read?

Were you read to as a child? What do you remember of that experience?

What stands out as your favorite or most influential book, the one that left you feeling betrayed because you hoped it would never end but did! Did you think, "I could do that."

Did anyone ever tell you should be a writer?

Answer them with a paragraph or two as if you are speaking to just one person.

Lesson 1:

Approximating

Writing is not about finding your inner child; it's about finding your inner adult. Kids play in a sandbox. Adult writers play in the desert, usually a sandstorm away from the Great Pyramids of Egypt. You are the archaeologist of your own unique history, the one buried by trauma or encapsulated by a good life that numbed you to the world around you. You dig until you find your name in the hieroglyphics of a sarcophagus with a facsimile of your face tooled upon it. After you gulp at recognition, you realize that you really *do* have a story that only you can tell. Your history is your exclusive property, to share as memoir or morph into fiction.

Fiction?

In Ken Kesey's *One Flew Over the Cuckoo's Nest* (the novel, not the corrupted movie) we know from page one that Chief Broom has all his faculties; playing deaf and dumb is his useful masquerade. He is our narrator. On page three, he tells us "… If you knew what went on in here, if I told you what went on in here, you'd think I was crazy, but it's the truth, even if it didn't happen."

Fiction is the truth, even if it didn't happen.

Janet Malcolm, born Jana Wienerová in my favorite city in the world (Prague, of course) in 1934 and still going strong at 86 has written for *New Yorker Magazine* since 1963. She appears to side with the Chief:

> "In a work of non-fiction, we almost never know the truth of what happened. The ideal of unmediated reporting is achieved only in fiction ... the writer faithfully reports what is going on in his imagination."

You probably tend to write in the same genre as the books you like to read. Yet, even sci-fi or Harlequin Romances can address existential questions. There is nothing, really, that prevents writing in any genre from elevating into the realm of literary fiction. But what is literary fiction? Easy answer. *The Old Man and the Sea* is not about fishing.

There is one truism worth acknowledging here: Rather than learn the tricks of the trade, learn the trade. Regardless of the books that most inspire your determination to write, be it *War and Peace* or *It*, flexing your mastery of principles presented in this book are mandatory.

According to Lily Tomlin, what separates us from the lower animals is the desire to do drugs. Before toying with the catnip, consider something else: humans communicate with symbols. There are of course animals that communicate very well with one another, but that is *vocal*, not *verbal*. "Don't mess with my kids or I may end up calling the police. In fact, I may dispense with you myself as I have a loaded gun in my purse. And I bite, weigh close to 800 pounds, and my claws are quite sharp. You should be, therefore, afraid of me, and follow my suggestion. Don't mess with my kids." A wonderful, declarative statement. Lacking language but having a voice box, a bear can communicate all that with one, mighty, bad-breath *R-O-A-R!* And you *won't* mess with her kids!

So, we humans are at a disadvantage. As writers, we can't convey the implications of body language, which may account for 70% of human-to-human communications. What we convey to one another is generally accomplished with words, a translation of feeling and thought and attitude before it even leaves our lips, to be further interpreted by our intended listener or reader. But what we *do* get in compensation is the power of *nuance*. The symbols of speech—vocabulary—and the way we string words together, allows us to convey nuance of thought and feeling that as far as we know evades mother bears, rabbits, and orangutans (not sure about dolphins and whales). We can even coach the reader on how to interpret those words: He spoke *softly*/she answered *defiantly*.

But still, we can only *approximate* understanding an author's intent. Be aware *your* reader can only approximate *your* intent. Here is a simple little experiment, one you may already have tried yourself: Define "love." And then try to find even *one* other person who defines it as you do. Get back to me if you find a match.

When you begin to write your story, do not deceive yourself into thinking that people will understand you. The best that you can hope for is that you come close enough in composing the arrangement of words on a page to *approximating* what you think or feel so that your reader can approximate the same experience.

Describe what your kitchen, or more to the point, what the kitchen in your manuscript looks like. No matter how much detail you include, it will not be the kitchen that your reader sees. They will translate your words into their own version of kitchen, which you've implanted as the setting in which a dialogue or action is about to take place. But use common sense. If you describe a kitchen in Asia of fifty years ago, no garbage disposals or Waring Blenders. Clay pots, bok-choy, wooden spoons, woks—and don't forget the scents that pervade the air. You might not want the smell of bacon frying in a Kibbutz.

Stainless steel kitchen sink? Not a lot of room for misinterpretation. But now, imagine the difficulty of conveying something abstract, like how your protagonist felt when their father died, or their daughter was born. You are counting on your reader to have had the same or compatible experience of equivalent emotional depth that they can transpose to grasp the feeling you so urgently want them to share.

And that's what makes *metaphor* indispensable. More than any other arrow in your quiver, metaphor allows you to offer a concept, a vision, that does not require exactitude, and allows the* reader to be a participant in your story, rather than a passive observer, because you are giving them the GIFT of using their own imagination and to take over your story, *elevating your role from that of scribe to guide*. I could very easily have said "More than any other writer's device …." But using metaphor—in this case, *arrow in your quiver*—gives you the same information, but in a way that is a more engaging, less-likely-to-fall-asleep way. (*Would personalizing "the reader" to "*your* reader" more fully engage you?)

Reading is a constant act of interpretation/translation. "She was a beautiful woman" will have your reader conjuring up their own prejudices about what constitutes beauty.

Her eyes were   *brown, and almond shaped, her lashes long.* (factual)
or
Her eyes were   *the portal to everything he desired in a woman.* (equally factual)

But which sentence is more engaging? There is nothing wrong if you prefer sentence number one, but the second sentence allows *the/your* reader to fill in the blanks. What is everything your protagonist desires in a woman, that *your reader* desires in a woman? Portal implies entry. Entry to what? Her life? Her pleasures? Her hidden thoughts? Or, let's go for the cliché: Her soul? (By the way, it is too contrived for me to try to remain pc, gender-attuned all the time as I write. In fact, I give up on the idea. I am male: his/her life, his/her pleasures, his/her soul? Preferring a masseuse to a masseur does not make me massagyinistic.) You might consider your editor a masseur, massaging a deep-tissue story out of you. Hmnn ... it's appropriate here to tell you why I want your manuscript on my table.

Ahhh ... There's the rub.

Then, the world beckoned ....

Why I am an Editor

I was the skinny kid with glasses who held the jacket when somebody with more balls than me had had enough and was going to punch somebody's lights out in the playground after school. I observed the passions—sometimes volatile passions—of life's real participants, from the safety of the sidelines.

I lived my adventures for the longest time vicariously, a type b, lower case, ten-point font, in a world intimidated by type A's, bold, maybe even italicized and underlined, 24-point Franklin Gothic Heavy.

Then the world beckoned, and I dabbled in high risk, exposing first myself and eventually my family to unconscionable danger (such as paying a smuggler to get us across the Straits of Malacca in a sampan at two in the morning after the gunboats passed).

One day while shaving I saw the first lines penciling across my forehead, and then I knew it; I wasn't holding somebody else's jacket anymore, and somewhere along the line I stopped living my life like a turtle crossing a highway.

Though retelling my (mis)adventures can hold anybody's attention for a half an hour at a dinner party, I know the best stories are the ones that take place under the skin.

Tell me a story about climbing Mount Everest, and I'm already bored. I know what it's all about. You climb. There is risk. You almost die. You have an epiphany. You come down off the mountain. You write a book about it.

BUT … tell me how you screwed up your marriage(s). Tell me what went wrong, what *you* did wrong. Tell me how your youngest daughter ended up in prison, and why it should be you in her place. Tell me of the insurrections that you yourself led with every relationship that ever meant anything to you, who you wanted to murder, and why. Who wanted to murder you, and why. Tell me of sabotage and heresy and destruction and betrayal and mutiny, redemption and infinite "second" chances and of pain and of pleasure and fury, and the *joy* you carved out for yourself in spite of it all. Tell me these things, and you have my attention, and I will hold your jacket after school in the playground. Old habits die hard.

I became an editor because *you* have a story, yet to be told.

I'm listening.

———

"Thornton Sully is one of the best editors I've ever worked with. Before I met Thorn, I retained a well-respected and highly recommended editor to red-line my manuscript. It took her several months and the results were helpful, but not what I was looking for. So, when Thorn brought up the idea of sending the first few pages of my manuscript to him to review for free, I was hopeful, but didn't expect much. I'm so glad I sent them over. I learned more in two pages from him than I did on the entire manuscript from the other editor! The quality jumped up markedly …. I didn't always agree with everything he said, but the way he said it never got my back up, which is an art in itself."

Laura Roser, *CEO Legacy Arts Magazine*

Your first discovery as an editor should not be too surprising: your clients want your approval. You have become or will become their confidant. It's part of the job description.

This tremendous honor brings with it tremendous responsibilities. To be an editor you must first be a writer; you must know first-hand the anguish of trying to structure a story without pissing away its adrenaline or becoming the Yellow Pages: perfect, and perfectly boring. To be a better editor, become a better writer.

Hesitant to take advice from strangers?

As Woody Guthrie said, "Take it easy ... but take it."

LESSON 1:

Approximating

WORKOUT

Assignment: In the context of this chapter, "Define love" is a rhetorical question, planted in the text to make the point that communicating an emotion, idea, or social construct is far more difficult than describing something material, like a kitchen sink. Here's a worthwhile analogy. The late Dr. Dan Casriel, the revolutionary psychiatrist who fostered the development of Primal Therapy, shared his observation with me that you cannot define what a healthy person is, you can only describe the *characteristics* of a healthy person, and he goes on to list about eight of them. A healthy person is both creative and productive. A healthy person can let go of any relationship that is destructive to their well-being. A healthy person will start each day anticipating the best. And so on.

You cannot define what a writer is, but you can list attributes of those who write. Chief among those? A writer is intensely curious about the motives that drive other people's behavior. A writer is a fastidious observer of events, interactions between people.

> "It has been said there are only nine different human faces on earth, while there are no two snowflakes alike. This is not to say the limited cannot observe the infinite."
>
> Mike Stang

A writer consumes the details of his surroundings, with all his senses. A writer collates these details in a physical journal or in his mind and can recreate them to support his storytelling. *A writer has fire in the belly*. A writer believes that his vision is unique and will vanish if he doesn't commit it to the back of a napkin before he leaves *Einstein's Bagels* or the Café Louvre, in Prague, where the *other* Einstein, along with Max Brod and Franz Kafka would drink cappuccino and flirt with the waitresses, circa 1912.

Café Louvre, Prague

(Franz: I have a Trial to attend to. Shouldn't we be more productive with our time?)

(Albert: It's all relative. Pass me that roach.)

Sound like you?

So, this assignment is to interview three people. Ask them to define what love is. I'm sure everyone you interview will have thought about this often in their lives. A latent benefit of this exercise is to give you the hint of what an editor does, which is to encourage his authors to think deeply, and express themselves convincingly.

I suggest you interview subjects that could not be of any romantic interest to you, as they might misconstrue your motives. Interview someone of the same gender if you are heterosexual; interview a couple; interview someone in a retirement home. I am not sure which author I am paraphrasing, but most people don't listen to others in order to understand them; they listen to prepare their own response. Be aware of this foible.

A little foreplay leading to the question "Define love" might include these warm-ups:

When was the last time someone told you they loved you?

How old were you when you first fell in love?

Do you ever imagine what your first love is doing now, and if they ever think of you?

You're not conducting a survey, and you're not a census taker; you're someone genuinely interested to hear the perspective of a fellow inhabitant of Planet Earth. You are initiating a conversation. A novel is a conversation in which dialogue is but one component.

Flex your writerly muscles in this exercise. You're gathering information, not disseminating it.

LESSON 2:

Masterpiece Sentences

Now, let me tell you *how* I became an editor. I started writing book reviews for the San Diego Union Tribune 20 years ago, and just by chance a number of the books I reviewed were novels in the time frame of the Civil War. I was intentionally kind in my reviews, knowing that if someone got published, Simon and Schuster or Random House saw something in an author's manuscript worthwhile, and it was incumbent upon me to see what that was. I was never brutal in my reviews. Even if I thought a book failed to achieve its purpose, I would try to find something redemptive within the manuscript, especially with new writers still testing their chops. But I knew that one day I would find a piece of work that *was* a piece of work, in which an author forgot the *primary rule* of writing a novel: *The song is always more important than the singer.* That was my line in the sand. Sure enough, one author's outsized ego swamped the story he wanted to tell. I was so offended by his vanity, injecting himself as the (anti)hero of his own novel and thinking we wouldn't see through it that I let him have it, and concluded my review with a line that the author made a Manassas of himself, a battlefield littered with dead clichés.

Got an email about three days later: "I read your review. I myself have a novel of the Civil War and would not like to suffer the same fate. I'll pay you $1,000 to read my manuscript and give me an opinion." Shortly thereafter, I discovered how energizing it was to be involved with writers with a story to tell, and to help them develop their skills. I want to help you develop yours, and this next exercise will help. You can do this with a writing partner if you like.

As a prelude to this exercise, read this adequate but bland sentence:

> *He walked down a flight of steps and felt into the breast pocket of his overcoat for cigarettes, even before he reached the glass door in the foyer.*

A Flexercise: Diagnose and then administer steroids

What can you speculate about this character from this single sentence?

1) He lives (or is visiting someone) in an apartment building. Foyer almost exclusively indicates a residence, while lobby would more than likely denote a professional building. Do you live in a house? When you cross over the threshold, do you step into your foyer or your lobby? If it were a professional building, he would probably be exiting from an elevator rather than by a flight of stairs.
2) It is fall or winter, based on wearing an overcoat.
3) He is probably an executive of some kind, or at least white collar, because he has an overcoat, rather than sweater or pullover or sweatshirt or jacket.
4) It is probably a city, evidenced by the door being glass. A rural setting would have a wooden door.
5) Reaching for cigarettes indicates stress, especially when you add the word "even" before, indicating urgency.
6) Stumbling or staggering could indicate any number of things, from fatigue to hangover or being drunk or agitated or being in a hurry. These possibilities are not suggested if he "walked" down a flight of steps.
7) "felt into his breast pocket" is also neutral.

See how the possibilities change if the sentence is:

He staggered down a flight of steps and groped the breast pocket of his overcoat for his Gauloises, even before he confronted the glass door in the foyer.

 And what more can we speculate about him if we know the brand of cigarettes? We are probably in Europe. Gauloises are manufactured in France; in fact, the name translates to "French women." The brand is especially strong, probably without filters. Is he a bit of a rogue? The harsh smokes might imply this. What if what he reaches for instead is his pipe? What if instead of calling it a pipe we call it his meerschaum?

What if it's a joint?

He did not "reach" the door—he confronted it. This could indicate he is of a combative nature, or maybe feels the world is stacked against him, if something as neutral as an exit to a building is cause for confrontation.

For our writer's exercise, see if you can rewrite the following sentences to put your personal stamp on them and make it more interesting. (Or rather than saying "more interesting," what if I said, "add some minced garlic to them?" Doesn't that better convey what you must do?)

He/she set his/her glasses on the table after reading an interesting article in the Wall Street Journal/Hustler/National Enquirer/Stern and called over the waiter.

There is *so-o-o* much to unpack here: multiple directions the story can go, and so much we already know about the subject. But fill in what kind of table. Dining, coffee table, bar? Stern is a German paper. Is he in Germany, or in Manhattan wanting to get the news of home? After you have completed a sentence with the parameters given, hand it to somebody and ask them to tell you as much as they can about your character.

Marguerite opened the refrigerator and plucked the Chardonnay from the door.

Knows enough that Chardonnay is best chilled. Refinement implied. "Plucked" implies nimble, agile; hence, youthful. She is in her own home, because she was not looking to see if there was wine, but knew it was in the door. The bottle is stored vertically. What can that imply? Probably middle class or upper middle class. Rich would imply either a wine cellar, or a wine cooler, and wine stored horizontally. Rewrite the sentence as if it is the first line to your novel, your first chance to pull in your reader. You could add a detail, such as "with her bandaged hand," or "before the zombies broke down the door." But subtlety is always appreciated!

Jacob made it all the way to the car before he realized he left the stove on.

We know without saying it that what he left was his house or apartment, and that he is probably preoccupied in some important thought. Or you could add: "[…] stove on and locked himself out." Instant conflict!

As you rewrite these sentences, see how much information you can convey to a reader, done by inference. Don't bludgeon them over the head with details, rather, allow them to participate in your story by letting them fill in the details themselves. Once you have done that, continue the story for a few paragraphs, focusing on how the action helps us know something of the personality of the subject.

LESSON 2:

Masterpiece Sentences

WORKOUT

Assignment: Write a book review of the last book you read, or, as an option, your *own* book. Imagine the task was assigned not by me, but by a major newspaper. The implication is that there is a deadline that can't be missed, and a word count that can't be violated. Qualifying that, it is a common practice to actually ADD 20% to the text if the piece is to appear in hard print (remember what a newspaper used to be?) so the editor has the option of having something to trim or expand, depending on the page layout on which the review will appear. Usually, I would assert which parts of the text should be the first to sacrifice, to put on the chopping block if necessary. Let's give your review a 600-word limit, meaning a draft that is roughly 720 words. Highlight the 20% you would first omit if called upon to do so. An aside: Typically, I tell a client, after they have submitted to me what they consider their final draft, to surgically *remove* 20%. You do this either by liposuction—deleting whole sections—or by what we refer to as "death by a thousand cuts," pinpricks or incisions to bleed out isolated words in each sentence that in the end may be superfluous. And guess what? If you delete them and the sentence still rings true, they *were* superfluous.

My editor at the time told me that what I was being paid for was an *opinion*, not a summary of events. I commented on the subject matter only to give context to the writer's ability to engage his reader. I was usually given six weeks, enough time to read the book twice, write, review, edit, and write again. My personal trademark was to inject vernacular consistent with the theme of the book. My review of a Civil War novel, *The Widow of the South*, included language such as (referring to the writer's attempt to weave in a love story) "This too, would prove to be an uphill battle." A review of the non-fiction about Western expansion, *Coyote Warrior: One Man, Three Tribes, and the Trial that Forged a Nation.*

[...] "Coyote Warrior" is more than just a recitation of injustices longer than a train of Conestoga wagons (tres)passing westward across the rolling plains; it is the striking of flint in the tall grass in yet another hillock of American claims of high moral ground.

The essence of the review is to give your reader reason to head to Barnes and Noble or the digital world of Amazon, or to persuade them their time would be better spent gardening. If you are reviewing your own book, remember that this is not a query letter; your intention is not to sell your manuscript, tempted as you may be, but to enlighten your reader.

LESSON 3:

He said/She said:

Attribution and the Ballad of Jack and Jill

Attribution is the means by which you inform your reader who is speaking. This should not be considered a rote task. How you accomplish this offers you an opportunity to be creative, with the underlying assumption that the more creative you are, the more likely you are to achieve your ultimate goal: to keep your reader turning pages.

Generally, you only physically identify the speaker if the reader would be confused about who is speaking. There is usually very little difficulty if there are only two people involved; let's call them Jack and Jill.

In this set up it's clear who starts the conversation:

After three rings, Jill picked up the phone.
"Hey, it's me. Did you make it to the concert?"
"No. I missed the last bus."
"That's a pity. The conductor dropped the baton."
"I have never known that to happen."
"Pure chaos."
"I feel sorry for the guy."
"Actually, it was a woman. Helen Kunderkova."
"Oh, dear."
"She might have been drinking."
"I've heard rumors."
"So have I."
"Are you coming over?"

Because of the multiple exchanges, even though there are only two speakers, you could get confused as to who is speaking. If you give just one reference to attribution, you have hit the reset button. You can use your own judgment where to apply it, and whether you are going to do so in the most conventional way (he said, she said, Jack said, Jill said, or any number of words: answered, replied, continued, etc.) OR (preferred method, because it interjects ACTION—even a sigh is action) you can identify the speaker in a more intriguing way. The line *"Oh, dear"* could be expanded.

"Oh, dear. Hang on. You caught me just as I was coming through the door. Let me set the groceries down."

Without naming her, we know it is Jill by the set-up: Jack has called her. Jack is not setting down groceries.

A compatible approach could be:

"Oh, dear." Jill switched to speaker while she set the wine in the fridge/ let out the cat/turned on the fan/fireplace.

BONUS! The activities that you use for attribution can further define/ flesh out your character. Jill has a cat (what kinds of people have cats?), likes wine and, because it is going in the fridge, it is probably white, and has turned on the fan/fireplace, maybe indicating the season?

Now, here are the same sentences, overpopulated with conventional attribution:

After three rings, Jill picked up the phone.
"Hey, it's me. Did you make it to the concert?" asked Jack.
"No. I missed the last bus," Jill replied.
"That's a pity. The conductor dropped the baton," Jack remarked.
"I have never known that to happen," remarked Jill.
"Pure chaos." Jack added.
"I feel sorry for the guy," commiserated Jill.
"Actually, it was a woman. Helen Kunderkova," Jack clarified.
"Oh, dear," Jill sighed.
"She might have been drinking," Jack suggested.
"I've heard rumors," concurred Jill.
"So have I," Jack acknowledged.
"Are you coming over?" Jill queried.

You can easily see how tedious this becomes. In the sentence *"Actually, it was a woman."* We know it is Jack speaking, and we know by the action that he is *clarifying*. Same thing with the sentence: *"She might have been drinking."* We know it's Jack speaking, and we see he is *suggesting*. Similar comments could be made regarding each of the sentences in this sample.

Now, seeming to contradict myself, there ARE at least two instances when you want to give attribution even if you know who is speaking. The first is to slow down the dialogue, which you might want to do if you have just delivered or are about to deliver something significant, and you want the thought to linger a moment with your reader before you continue. Expanding our dialogue with Jack and Jill and assuming there has been minimal direct attribution up to this point:

> *"So have I."*
> *Jill hesitated before tapping off-speaker and bringing the phone to her ear. "Are you coming over?"*

There is some trepidation on her part (as implied by switching off the speaker and being physically more intimate with the phone). It's your story. Why is she hesitant? Is she afraid he will say no? Why? Is she afraid he will say yes? Why? You are setting up conflict, which drives every story. And you are suggesting there are secrets—always good to have and keep as long as possible.

The second reason you might want to give attribution where technically none is needed is to convey emotion, if the emotion is not already clear by the setting or action of the scene.

> *"Are you coming over?" she said/angrily, seductively, annoyingly, softly/ curiously.*

But try giving the same information without "she said/asked/pleaded."

> *"Are you coming over?" What was the date of my last period?/Of course he's coming over, that freeloader. Can't pass up a free meal/ She grit her teeth, certain the answer would disappoint her.*

By the way—someone's thoughts are always put in italics, rarely in quotation marks.

The best writing, of course, identifies who is speaking without any concrete attribution at all. The voice (literal and metaphorical) of each character is so distinct from others that we know who is speaking. One is college educated, speaks in full sentences, grammar always correct, sentences often compound. Another character is a street waif, short, incomplete sentences. The military guy likes monosyllabic, straight-to-the-point sentences, declarative sentences, and frequently uses the word "outstanding." The tall-dark-and-handsome uses very few words (he doesn't need to!). Somebody has a stammer, another a lisp, another a Southern accent. The narcissist makes frequent references to himself and uses superlatives. One coughs. Multiple hints to give attribution without being direct.

Now, one more thing about attribution: mix it up where it appears in the dialogue. In this example, we don't need attribution at all, but in sentences of your own where it may be required, apply these as possibilities:

Example One

"Hey, it's me. Did you make it to the concert?" asked Jack.
"No. I missed the last bus," Jill replied.
"That's a pity. The conductor dropped the baton," Jack remarked.

Example Two

"Hey, it's me. Did you make it to the concert?" asked Jack.
Jill replied. "No. I missed the last bus."
"That's a pity. The conductor dropped the baton," Jack remarked.

Example Three

Jack asked, "Hey, it's me. Did you make it to the concert?"
"No. I missed the last bus," Jill replied.
Jack remarked, "That's a pity. The conductor dropped the baton."

Example Four

"Hey, it's me." Jack asked, "Did you make it to the concert?"
"No. I missed the last bus," replied Jill.
"That's a pity," remarked Jack. "The conductor dropped the baton."

I'm sure you get the idea. If you can avoid syntactical patterns, you will create a more spontaneous read. Remember the great paradox: *write something a hundred times until it appears to be spontaneous!*

The one fallback word to use for attribution, if you must? SAID. It is direct, doesn't distract from the conversation or leave you interpreting motives so you can focus on the action and dialogue.

Jack and Jill went up the hill
To fetch a pail of water.
*At least, that's what they **said** they did,*
But now they've got a daughter.

I guess they had their own special bucket list.

"And these are the thoughts that come to mind when I think about attribution," Thorn *said*.

LESSON 3:

He said/She said

WORKOUT

Assignment: As kids, my cousins were caught smoking behind the barn. My uncle's solution was to make each of them smoke a cigar down to the nubs, inhaling every puff. They got sick, of course, and threw up, and neither of them took up smoking as an adult.

In this exercise, create 20 lines of dialogue, and after each character speaks, repeat their name and follow it with *replied, answered, admonished, commented, indicated, whispered, cried, shouted.* But no using the word *said.* AND you can only use two of the words in the list! Creative application of attribution is so important, such an incredible opportunity to flavor your manuscript, I don't want you smoking when you reach adulthood!

While I have just *commented, indicating* that some things are best left *unsaid*, this is worth repeating: Enroll now in the Interactive Course that supplements the text. This will allow you to turn in your assignments for professional feedback and guidance, and what you invest in yourself now you'll recoup later. The total course fee is deductible when you purchase blocks of time to have me work with you editing your novel, once you have a working knowledge of the principles in *Fire in the Belly*. Here's the link with details:

https://gumroad.com/l/IPaVR

LESSON 4:

Manicure your Manuscript

Rubbing Aladdin's Lamp:
What a developmental editor does

Consider your story as vapor imprisoned within a magic lantern, and the editor, once he gets his hands on it, rubs until the genie materializes from the haze. Your story may have been building up pressure inside your lantern or lurking behind your computer screen for years. Probably needs a bath, maybe a shave and manicure before it meets the general public. Maybe even dental work and a wardrobe change before the debutante ball.

©.Disney productions

That's when the *developmental* editor puts on a pot of coffee. They are the person with whom you are sharing your most outrageous thoughts or most intimate secrets, a.k.a. your manuscript. Of the several types of editing venues, this is the one that requires the most personal interaction. Proofreading will follow, but only after you and your editor (yes, use the possessive: *your* editor) agree that your story has reached its potential.

The cardinal rule for a developmental editor is to swear in blood that you are the world's leading authority on your own story. Their job is to help you tell that story in the most persuasive way.

Persuasive is a good word choice here. Isn't your manuscript, in its broadest sense, an attempt to persuade your readers of something? Maybe the importance of an event or an experience, or of an observation you've documented, maybe even discovered, about the human condition?

Don't go to bed on the first date. Give a prospective editor a few pages, even a chapter, to see what sort of comments they offer. Do their comments resonate? Google the editor. Ask them for testimonials from other clients.

A developmental editor helps you navigate strategic choices, as well. I was given a manuscript by a Vietnam veteran who announced on page one that his best friend, Herman, died in his arms in battle, and then went on to describe how they loved each other, shared adventures and fears, dope and hope, and how it grieved him when Herman died.

Without really changing the story, we agreed to let readers develop a relationship with Fred (the author) and with Herman before the tragedy, so that when Fred felt the loss, so did the readers, who by midway in the book surely had developed a fondness themselves for both men. There is much more to this story, and, miraculously, an unimaginably happy ending, but I'll save that for a bit later.

The book, *Raw Man*, by Fred Rivera, became the winner of the Isabel Allende Miraposa Award for best new fiction at the International Latino Literacy Awards.

What is most important is to bring on an editor early in the process. It can save you tons of grief if the editor can spot anything problematic, so you don't repeat it as you surge ahead with your writing.

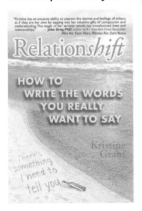

One authoress of a non-fiction vacillated from being conversational to formal: "One should always/ you should always." By helping her understand that her self-help book was really a conversation with women, her writing became much more relaxed and effective. The quality of her thoughts had not changed; they were just presented in a way more likely to help her get the outcome she was after. In the final draft of *Relationshift: How to write the words you really want to say*, authoress Kristine Grant spoke directly to her audience, and changed the tone from being declarative to involving them in a conversation. So, "One should always" became "What would you think if …" This is typical of a way in which a developmental editor prepares you to go public. Imagine the opening line in Moby Dick: "One should call me Ishmael." Abstract, cranial. "Call me Ishmael" invites you inside the story with just three words.

Another client developed a habit of starting an inordinate number of sentences with "But." A word search revealed the use of "but" 1,700 times in a 100,000-word manuscript. Either as a conjunction or to begin a sentence. And of course, the use of the word "but" has a tendency to negate everything that preceded it. That can become pretty enervating after a while. This was detectable within the first 30 pages, and had the author been aware of how distracting it was, he could have saved himself some grief by putting on his scrubs and sterilizing his scalpel. (I am pleased to say the author's diligence paid off. Mark Cohen is now shopping his wonderfully engaging *Listening to the Echo* to an agent.*) If you seem to notice you use a word or phrase with a bit too much frequency, do a word search and you'll see just how much. Seeing the actual count may be enough to cause you to download a thesaurus.

---

* Mark shares a bit of his process to find an agent.

"Trying to find an agent is like going through AA or NA (depending on your addiction). You have to work the steps, and it takes time. I've been working the steps. I'd say it took me about a year to get my query letter to the point where I think I have a chance of attracting an agent. Though, I'm still making refinements.

I've sent out about ten or so query letters since my new and improved model, but no bites yet. For each agent that I identify as a possibility, I do a background search. I take a look at the books an agent has sold and, in some cases, read one or more of the books. I read and watch agent interviews that I locate. I look at an agent's Facebook page and Twitter feed. I'm looking for a hook that I can put in the first paragraph of my query letter that explains why I am contacting the particular agent. On average, it takes me about ten days from when I first identify an agent to when I send out my query letter.

Just yesterday I entered three short story contests, all with January 31st deadlines. The story I had entered is an excerpt from my novel. I had to make some modifications so that the excerpt reads like a short story. I also sent my novel to Schaffnerawards.com. Schaffner is an independent publisher that sponsored a contest for music-related novels.

The Jewish Book Council (https://www.jewishbookcouncil.org/) has 92-page list of books that I am still going through. I try to identify books that have some similarities to *Listening to the Echo*. I then attempt to find out who represents the author. From that point, I research the agent to see if he or she may be fit for my novel."

But I digress! The takeaway is this: most people who are teasing out their first work-in-progress are only vaguely aware of how an editor can help them. A classic Catch-22: if they realized they needed an editor from the beginning of their project they would have one, and, of course, if they don't engage an editor, they *don't* realize this. If you are an editor, then it must certainly appear to be self-serving to tell potential client that they need you. But they do. A writer provides vision, but an editor provides clarity. "Sometimes you do not hear your own thoughts until someone else says them."—Lucien Zell.

My experience among my peers, those writers who have become editors, is that there is an abundance of generosity of time and encouragement before money is even broached. We are excited by the prospect of discovering a really good writer and doing our part to encourage their endeavors. If you are nursing a work-in-progress or even an uninitiated concept, perhaps this little intervention on my part will persuade you to do what professionals do: establish a relationship with an editor who can course-correct rather than repair your manuscript.

A novice writer would not have cause to understand that there are different types of editors, each with distinct functions, that sometimes intersect, but generally come sequentially. Your first close encounter of the word kind will be with the developmental editor. Rarely does the developmental editor offer you a fixed price based on your word-count, though it is reasonable to get a fixed price (usually per page) for proofreading, which does not require an intimate relationship between author and editor.

Here is a little exercise for you. Write a half a page documenting the origins of your understanding that the time to hire an editor is after you have completed your first or final draft. Where did that idea come from? Then, personify that mind-set. Give it a name. Harold? Then plot and execute Harold, freeing yourself of him forever and the dis-service he imposed upon you. And while you're at it, plot the assassination of Eleanor, or whoever told you that you could never be as good a writer as the one you admire most.

Your client is absolutely certain their words coherently and passionately convey what they think and feel; your job as a developmental editor will be to break it to them gently if that's not true, and then offer suggestions of how to correct what's coarse and to course-correct. We all think we are perfect lovers, sometimes taken aback when our lover offers a little coaching. Confess. Aren't you glad they did? It's not a bad analogy. We become better if the advice proffered is communicated thoughtfully and with the best intentions. The dance you will learn as an editor is to radiate confidence in your own judgment while concurrently expressing respect for your author's point of view. Practice makes poignant.

I had a manuscript in which the actions of the protagonist, a woman, were accurately described, and could only have been done so if the vision of the woman was clear in the author's mind as she wrote. But there was no physical description of the woman because the author was so wrapped up in telling the story that she did not realize the reader had no idea what her heroine looked like. It's easy to be oblivious when you're sucked into the vortex of writing with passion, and you're prepared to kill whoever is calling on the phone that you forgot to mute.

Catching small oversights like this are often easy fixes—sometimes just a few minutes, but a manuscript populated with small errors can undermine a great story. Errors of neglect can be just as crippling as errors embedded in the manuscript.

The value of having a mixed bag of real-world experiences can't be overstated. David was a client with the all-consuming hobby of getting behind the helm of anachronistic tall ships—the ones barrel-bodied with multiple masts and sails: barks and brigantines whenever the possibility allowed. He crafted a marvelous trilogy that drew heavily from his knowledge and experience, with much of the saga getting its sea-legs in centuries past. David wrote a thrilling scene in which mid-shipman Mason, his hero, must go aloft during a blistering tempest in the dark of night to reef in a sail, arduous and dangerous even under the best of weather conditions.

The wind is horrific, blinding, and so strong—according to the first unedited draft—that it fills young Mason's cheeks as he opens his mouth to breathe while he labors. The problem with this description was that if he was reefing sails, that is, if he was gathering them up to secure to the spars to avoid the wind ripping them to shreds, it would be his *butt-cheeks* that would fill, as the wind would be coming from behind him, not in front of him! My modest background under sail made this immediately apparent.

Your own varied life experiences will better enable you to tag-team with your author. While you may not have similar tangible pursuits like this to draw from, if you have been on the planet for a while, you *will* have had multiple experiences—successes and failures—with human relationships that will better qualify you to assist your author as they shape the events of their own life into a story relatable, identifiable, to their readership.

All novels, after all, are about relationships. By the way, did I mention that **All novels, after all, are about relationships?**

An attorney does not necessarily have to believe his client in order to defend him. A developmental editor, sometimes called a *substantive editor*, by contrast, *must* believe in his client, and be his greatest advocate. Do you know the name of Tiger Woods' caddy? Neither do I. No one thinks less of Tiger Woods for absorbing feedback or soliciting advice from his caddy. In fact, everyone expects him to do so. Likewise, editor and author must each bring to their relationship a dose of humility and mutual admiration and respect if they are to collaborate to sink that final putt on the eighteenth chapter.

ALL FEATURES, GREAT AND SMALL

Less creative, but equally important, is the proofreader. Theirs is the exacting work; they don't choose your ensemble or color-coordinate suit and tie: they make sure your shirt is pressed or the pleats of the evening gown ironed before you make your formal appearance.

Spellcheck and programs like Grammarly tend to reduce the workload for a proofreader, but they are no substitute for a practiced eye. Did you mean "bear witness" or "bare witness?" Did you witness a bear meandering through the woods? Did you just come out of the shower naked and witness the accident through the window? Bear/bare with me; a proofreader will catch these eras. (A proofreader will also understand I meant "errors" and not "eras" which might fly under the radar of Spellcheck.) And should that period I just dropped down come before or after the parenthesis?

Just minor/miner details? Why is it important? Whatever it is you write, you are trying to persuade someone of something important to you. You lose them when you lose credibility. A professionally published manuscript littered with typos that pose or syntax that sins tells the reader that you lack the skills or dedication to present something unblemished. Furthermore, you want *nothing* to interrupt the flow of ideas from your pen. Each "little" flaw occupies space in the mind of your reader that should instead be filling up with the thoughts or feelings you want to share with them. A disagreement between noun and verb or switching from past to present tense can ignite a civil war on any page of your work, disrupting your story. Your developmental editor will probably catch most of this, as will a *line editor* or *content editor* but it is a proofreader with a different skill set who disarms the combatants and prepares you for print.

After I edited a very fine manuscript, its author was pleased to tell me, thinking he could save a few dollars, that his sister who teaches high school English would proofread it. "Fair enough," I told him. As we prepared to print, my curiosity got the better of me, and I combed over the manuscript myself and found 130 errors, all very subtle. (The professional standard for a printed book is fewer than four errors per 100,000 words.)

I assisted author Tracy Foust at the suggestion of her editor at Simon and Schuster with her memoir of growing up with obsessive compulsive disorder (OCD) titled "Nowhere Near Normal." An amusing irony? A case of that same disorder might have been a good thing at Simon and Schuster, as nobody noticed that the jacket to the hardcover was printed with the title "Nowhere Near Norman." Even the big kids make mistakes.

Similarly, a Pulitzer Prize-winner I work with submitted for ready-to-go publication a book in which the first page listed him as a *Pulizter* Prize-winner. An error hiding in plain/plane site/sight.

You have invested time, and probably a bit of blood and money in your manuscript. Maybe sleepless nights, too. Work an extra couple of shifts to pay for the services of a prooofreader, who will see that your fine effort is free of typos and arrows of spacing, grammar, spelling, syntax and such. (Did I mean errors?)

LESSON 4:

Manicure your Manuscript

WORKOUT

Assignment: I want you to create a scene. Two characters, a desk between them. One is a fledgling writer with his first completed manuscript, which he believes is good to go, except for maybe a bit of proofreading, and an ambiguous "polishing." He's already spending his royalty checks on a time-share in Cabo, after the mere formality of getting published. The one sitting behind the desk, a view of Manhattan behind him, is you, an editor he found on YELP. You have read his manuscript, and found it weak, amateurish. Begin the conversation, and you, the editor, must impart inspiration, knowing the manuscript in its current state is flat, though, if properly positioned under the leg, would stabilize the picnic table on your uneven patio near the barbeque of your Connecticut home. You are limited to speaking truth only. Your client will know if you're blowing smoke up his orifice. Save your client, save his manuscript, and earn your money. Two pages.

LESSON 5:

The Info-dump

One of the first orders of business in your novel is to establish time and place, to give your reader a footing in your story. It's also your very first opportunity to lull your reader to sleep, and the first dose of Ambien is the info-dump, which could be described as directly unloading information you want your reader to have, but without foreplay or finesse, or a thoughtful integration into your manuscript. Simply: dumped. It can occur anywhere in your manuscript, and is fatal if it occurs at the beginning. I was handed a manuscript to work with that began with:

> *"It was December ninth, 1941, two days after Pearl Harbor."*

Oh.

Using information I clawed from the first few pages, we morphed into this:

> *"Chief Petty Officer Andrew Parker drew long and hard from his cigarette. He thought he had kicked the habit, but the urge was too strong and it seemed trivial now, in the scheme of things. Huddled with his wife over the radio, they each listened in disbelief just one day earlier as his Commander-in-Chief let the words linger in the hall of Congress and crackle on the radio waves:*
>
> > *"... 'a day that will live in infamy' ..."*

Every reader literate enough to pick up your book will know that date, and the quote, and the time frame is further reinforced by listening to a radio—reminiscent of a by-gone time, when radio waves "crackled." Without specifics, we know it is America, because we have a chief petty officer, a Commander-in-Chief, and halls of Congress.

Maybe you know this one:

> *"This story takes place in France and England between 1775 and 1793."*

Did you remember to take your Viagra?

How about, instead:

"It was the best of times; it was the worst of times."

Again, I credit my reader to know this quote. If they don't, not too likely they'll be scouting for my books (or yours!) while perusing the aisles of Barnes and Noble. The title itself (I insult you if I think I have to tell you what it is) indicates the story plays out in two cities, clarified on the first page thusly:

> *"There were a king of large jaw and a queen with a plain face, on the throne of England; there were a king with a large jaw and a queen with a fair face, on the throne of France."*

So, before we have even a solidified date, we know it is a period of kings and queens. And finally, now that we are already in the setting and time frame, our suspicions are confirmed "It was the year of Our Lord seventeen-hundred and seventy-five." Would you have been drawn into the story if that had been the first line or would it bore the Dickens out of you?

(Thanks to artist Ruth Joyce, at ruthjoyce.com, creator of *Wuss'n'Boots*, for this gem of a gift 20 years ago!)

There is a commonly held belief that stories should not begin with references to weather. I disagree, because conditions of weather can be wonderful metaphorical statements. "It was the best of times, it was the worst of times, it was the age of wisdom, it was the age of foolishness, it was the epoch of belief, it was the epoch of incredulity, *it was the season of Light, it was the season of Darkness, it was the spring of hope, it was the winter of despair …*"

Here's another example from my own novel, *Almost Avalon*, of establishing time and place. The Yellow Pages, info-dump version would have been:

> *"This story (we already know it's a story) takes place on a boat at Catalina Island beginning one evening in December."*

You, or your editing client, is writing a novel, not a (confusing) assembly manual for Ikea or an invitation for a time share at Laurence Welk Village. You make a bargain between yourself and your reader when you publish a book: Pay me the money, and I will entertain you. Info-dumps are in violation of that agreement.

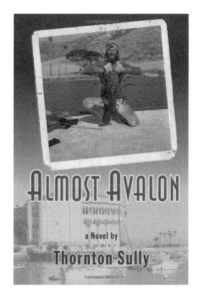

December tumbled out of a storm cloud one night passing over the island on its way to Los Angeles. (location already established … the island, not an island. I am giving my readers credit that they know the island off Los Angeles is Catalina.) *It **had** to have broken a few bones when it hit the deck,* (further refines the location: a boat) *and it woke me, but I didn't crawl out from under the blankets to investigate.* (confirms it is night) *I was hoping maybe I dreamed it, but there it was, early the next morning, cold and wet, pounding on the aft hatch, hungry, and telling me how it liked its eggs. It made itself comfortable, with no sign of moving on. I've been looking over my shoulder*

(On the deck of my boat at Cat Harbor. I'm the one with the beard. Available on Amazon)

for two weeks, and hiding the silverware since December made its descent. Tonight is no exception. December. It is the bully of all months, the disciple of the twelve to betray the good intentions of the calendar. It does not roll off the tongue, like April, or May. It scrapes the roof of your mouth to speak its name. Its voice is brittle and its words are harsh, and it berates my every move. (demonstrates the use of weather and seasons as metaphor) *"You're going to lose her, you know. Go back, while you still can. I'll make it easy for you. She'll understand."* (establishes that the story revolves around a heterosexual relationship, assuming—rightfully—that the narrator is male.)

Here's an example, halfway into the draft a client sent me, of an info-dump and how to correct it:

> "Dr. Bono, Chief of Staff of the Philadelphia Naval Hospital, was also a full-fledged navy captain. He greeted Dr. Rodriguez with a friendly salutation. "What brings you ashore? We both volunteered for sea duty when the South Dakota was first commissioned, and the last I heard you've remained aboard."

It is highly unlikely that in conversation Dr. Bono would have stated what both men already knew, and was history. In this info-dump scenario, the solution is fairly simple—you want the reader to have the information, but not dumped in unrealistic conversation, so:

> "What brings you ashore?" They had both volunteered for sea duty when the South Dakota was first commissioned. "The last I heard you remained aboard."

Here's a final example, though, as my editor, Arthur Salm at the San Diego Union Tribune enlightened me 20 years ago: "It's not final until it's in print." An editing client started her memoir riding in a car on the way to the courthouse to find out the disposition of her case. This was a good concept to launch her story, because it immediately established conflict. Win or lose the case? What would be the repercussions? And there is already tension in the air. Bonus points to you if you can make your reader feel something, *anything*, within your first few paragraphs.

But a needless info-dump undermined this good start and crippled her reader's hope that they were in the hands of a good story-teller about to tell a good story. Angela is sitting in the SUV staring at the doors to the courthouse, completely visible because leaves had fallen from all the trees. They'd passed dehydrating pumpkins on the stoops of rowhouses on their way. All good. We know without being told it's daytime, October/ November. A temperate climate that has seasonal changes. Probably middle America. Angela must be a woman of some substance because she drives an SUV instead of a Honda Civic, and can afford an attorney. Seems anti info-dumpy.

> "I waited for my attorney, John Harris, to come with news from the courthouse. John was a graduate of Harvard Law School."

Angela was trying to convey that she had a highly qualified lawyer representing her. Rather than making that info-dump statement, I encouraged a re-write where instead she simply had John espousing legalese in conversation. The simple act of sitting in her car watching the doors to the courthouse already establishes that she is "waiting." Telling us so is redundant.

They denied our motion for dismissal, is enough to establish at least by implication that John is an attorney. That impression is solidified as the conversation continues:

> "Does that leave us any options?"
> "I can make an appeal. The documents I submitted are *prima facia* evidence of intent by that bastard partner of yours to commit fraud. Harvard Law School Torts 101. I think somebody got to the judge. He should have recused himself. I'll move to have a change of venue to another jurisdiction. I'll run it by Larry."

All this implies experience and competence. *Running it by Larry* indicates John is in his element, connected to other lawyers, so he has been at this for some time. Much better than just saying John is an experienced lawyer with a Harvard Law degree.

The only place for an info-dump in a work of fiction is the author bio under your photo on the last page of your published novel.

LESSON 5:

The Info-dump

WORKOUT

Assignment: Convert this brief paragraph into something interesting to read:

Richard was a Caucasian male and Mildred was a Negro (using the vernacular of the times). They were married in June 1958. In Washington, D.C. They returned to their home in Virginia, a Southern State, (I slipped in this taboo, here; telling your reader that Virginia is a Southern State is something they know, and would feel it condescending for you to "inform" them of the fact. *Does he think we're stupid?*) and were arrested. "The Lovings were charged under Section 20–58 of the Virginia Code, which prohibited interracial couples from being married out-of-state and then returning to Virginia, and charged with Section 20–59, which classified miscegenation as a felony, punishable by a prison sentence of between one-and-five years." (Wikipedia)

While the way we are fed this information as non-fiction is appropriate, and we are riveted to the facts, if this were presented in a novel it would be a classic info-dump.

Convey this information as the start to your novel. Establish time without using the digital "1958." Establish they are married without saying they are married. Establish miscegenation is a felony without defining miscegenation. Establish they were arrested without saying they were arrested. (For example, they couldn't make bail.) Establish they drove to Washington D.C. to marry because it was illegal to wed in Virginia. The info-dump way of doing so would be, "Mildred, we have to drive to Washington, our nation's capital, because it is illegal for us to get married in Virginia and because their law says that people from different races are not allowed to get married, and you are a Negro and I am Caucasian, so we are of different races." (A bit over the top here to amplify my point.)

This exercise will require some thought and ingenuity on your part, but what *incredible* drama is contained in the premise! The Montagues and Capulets intent on thwarting true love! Romeo and Juliet denied their heart's desires! Richard and Mildred willing to defy the law and incur the wrath of a vengeful state to declare their love! The number one requirement of a novel is impossible conflict, the protagonist denied what they most fervently want! Insurmountable obstacles! Slay some dragons with this assignment. Careful … they, too, may have fire in the belly!

LESSON 6:

Sage Advice

My own quick perusal of the multiple sites that offer advice to editors and writers—new or not so new—seem to omit what I consider essentials. Make sure you don't neglect the gospel of Professor Ron McFarland, squeezer of better writing from students for over 50 years.

"My fundamental premise when it comes to writing papers for a 400-level English course is that no matter how proficient a writer you may be, you can probably get even better. This premise usually holds up pretty well for all but maybe 2 or 3 students in any given course. I may or may not mark your papers more closely than your other teachers do, but in any event, my hope is that you'll pay attention to what I've scribbled and will make some effort to profit from my well-meaning comments. What follows is a key, of sorts, to my procedures.

"When I think you have simply used a wrong word, given the context, I'll usually cross out what you've written and scrawl what I think is at least one correct option. When I think you've used a word that is okay but not very effective, I'll underline the word and jot down an option or two I think would be better.

"One of my peeves (I won't call it a 'pet' one) has to do with the proliferation of be-verbs, or verbs of being: is/are, was/were. I include the so-called expletive (there is/are, was/were) among these. The motive force, energy, and power of your sentences derives from active verbs. Example: There are many readers who might disagree with Hemingway's treatment of Marjorie in this story. Repair: Many readers might disagree with Hemingway's treatment of Marjorie in this story. Example: Nick's black eye is symbolic of the lessons he is about to learn about the harsh world. Repair: Nick's black eye symbolizes the lessons he is about to learn about the harsh world. In this case, the nominalization 'is symbolic of' is transformed into an active verb.

"You may already suspect I'm the sort of reader who does not much care for the verb feel/felt when it comes to your commentary and analysis. In general, so with think/thought. Nor do I cotton much to circumlocutions like 'it's my opinion that' when the simple statement 'I think' would be more exact and perhaps a little bolder.

"For whatever reason, I happen to be waging an undeclared war against the word 'that.' The word keeps popping up again and again in the writing of even some of my best students, and I also find myself getting sloppy with it. No way should 'that' recur three times in a typical sentence—you can almost always clip at least one of them, resulting in more concise phrasing. Some of the most irksome errors occur when it comes to punctuation, notably when quotations are involved. Simply put, in the US, periods & commas go inside quotation marks except when an in-text citation pulls them outside: Conklin claims Gatsby lies 'inevitably.' Conklin insists 'even Gatsby's war stories ring false' (42).

"I don't use many symbols other than *sp* for spelling, *pn* for punctuation, *cap* for capitalize, *l.c.* for lower case, and *agr* for agreement error (often accompanied by *s-v* for subject-verb or *n-p* for noun-pronoun). I do not accept the increasingly popular tendency to mate up singular nouns or pronouns that are gender neutral with plural pronouns: Anyone who disagrees with me is welcome to their opinion. Indeed, they are, but I will mark it every time. 'Anyone' (per the word 'one') is singular & requires a singular verb ('disagrees'); my logic indicates that 'anyone' requires a singular pronoun. One might rephrase as follows: Those who disagree with me are welcome to their opinion."

———•———

God wrote the law as ten commandments. Declined to hire an editor who might have been able to pare that down without losing the essence of the content. Probably afraid the Devil was in the details.

My mentor, the late author R.E. Harrington was able to edit the Laws of Novel Writing down to just *seven* commandments. Colored text is his.

R.E. Harrington's Laws of Novel Writing

Have Secrets: If you tell us everything, we will have no reason to go on reading.

Duh.

Create Interesting Characters: have them say and do fascinating things.

Create Conflict: have the characters want something they can't have.

Conflict is what drives your novel. I would venture to say that everyone reading *Fire in the Belly* already knows this, but you want to milk it for all its worth, because when the conflict ends, your novel is finished. A short mopping up is needed, the *post coitus* referred to as *denouement*, when you ask your reader, "Was it as good for you?" as they light a cigarette.

Write with Punch: ruthlessly trim useless adjectives, adverbs, and wordy dialogue.

To which I might add, spike the punch! That's my metaphorical way of sagely advising you to write without inhibition. As Ernest Hemingway never said, "Write drunk. Edit sober" (that was Peter DeVries). David Crosby was asked if he ever recorded anything while high. "I never recorded when I wasn't," and Leonard Cohen refers to "the visionary flood of alcohol."

I am not advocating that you lubricate your fingers with scotch or smoke Indian tobacco. Just let the horse you're straddling run free; the time to rein him in will follow.

My working title for what eventually became *The Boy with a Torn Hat* was *Striptease for the Blind*. Imagine a stripper on stage, cowering behind pink feather-boas, afraid to reveal her fear of revealing. Suddenly she learns that the entire audience is blind! No inhibitions! Free to experiment without fear of judgment! Literally literarily unedited.

John Steinbeck has my back on this.

"Write freely and as rapidly as possible and throw the whole thing on paper. Never correct or rewrite until the whole thing is down. Rewrite in process is usually found to be an excuse for not going on.

It also interferes with flow and rhythm which can only come from a kind of unconscious association with the material."

To which David Ogilvy adds:

"Big ideas come from the unconscious. This is true in art, in science, and in advertising. But your unconscious has to be well informed, or your idea will be irrelevant. Stuff your conscious mind with information, **then unhook your rational thought process.** You can help this process by going for a long walk, or taking a hot bath, or drinking half a pint of claret. Suddenly, if the telephone line from your unconscious is open, a big idea wells up within you."

Write in Active Voice: passive voice is usually enervating (look it up!).

Boil the Plot down to a Sentence or Two: use it as a guide.

A prerequisite I stipulate for each prospective editing client is that they tell me what their story is about in 30 words before we speak in person or on Zoom. "But WAIT! There's MORE!" is a common response. I don't ask that they be concise because I am collecting elevator pitches to sell on eBay or have limited time to read; I do it because it shows me the writer is focused and it sets the tone for being focused when we first meet. Anybody can tell me what their story is about if I allot them three pages. Harder than you think to capture the essence in just 30 words. Try it. And then I suggest that you print out those words and tape them just over your screen. This actually is advice that Robert Harrington gave me. You've got plenty of options and opportunities to add clay to the wheel, but as you start down a rabbit hole, ask yourself if what you are writing falls within the parameters that are staring at you just above your screen.

For example, let's say the hero of your story is racing, literally, to the hospital because he gets a call at the office that his wife is delivering their twins pre-maturely. Highway Patrol pulls him over. The officer, to your hero's thinking, is taking an excruciating amount of time to get out of the patrol car and give him a ticket. Tension builds! The babies, the babies! The wife! The babies!

The officer saunters over; maybe he decides that if someone is in such a hurry that they break the speed limit, why not administer a little extra-judicial punishment by dragging out the process of issuing a ticket? You are probably going to have your cop resemble the cliché: belly hangs over the belt, puts his hand on the holster of his gun, adjusts his sombrero, and lumbers like a Galapagos tortoise to the driver's window. Certainly not crisp and efficient. All this well and good. What we don't need is an explanation of what the cop had for breakfast or the argument he had with his wife that morning that makes him eager for a way to unleash a little hostility. I'm sorry if he didn't get any last night, but I really don't care. It's enough that we see he has stopped your protagonist from getting what he wants in a potentially life-and-death situation.

Write for 15 minutes a day.

Be careful! It's a trap! No writer can write for just 15 minutes a day. However, by *committing* to 15 minutes a day, you're vaccinated against writer's block—whose power is overrated—on the days that your muse is not amusing. Some successful writers commit themselves to a consistent number of hours each day, others to a consistent number of words or pages. *BUT all of them have a regimented routine from which they do not deviate!*

Jack London, who in his prime was the world's most read author, would only begin his day after he had written a thousand words. Stephen King has a quota of six pages a day, and the result is 50 completed novels, or thereabouts.

Hemingway is a bit more nuanced:

> "You read what you have written and, as you always stop when you know what is going to happen next, you go on from there. You write until you come to a place where you still have your juice and know what will happen next and you stop and try to live through until the next day when you hit it again."

No Pain, No Gain?

© La Commune Libre de Montmartre

Save that mantra for the gym. Writing is unmitigated pleasure. The quality of what you produce will not be enhanced if you happen to be suffering while you conjure up words to appear on your screen. The *recollections* you may draw from may be pain-inducing, but the writing, the act of creation, is not. I prefer Henry Miller's advice:

"Work calmly, joyously, recklessly on whatever is in hand."

One notable exception is my friend, best-selling author Victor Villaseñor, who is dyslexic and took a full six months to be able to write his first full page. Now in his eighties, Victor was a very angry young man, and he told me that writing was his way of getting even. (He also confided in me, "It's a good thing I got good at this. The only other thing I was good at was guns.)" After five years, he finally realized he actually *liked* to write!

Every successful writer that I know, and certainly everyone I have read about, ALL had a writing routine to which they adhered, even if their computer screen demurs, "Not tonight, dear, I have a headache." I suspect you are reading this *how-to* in the hope there is a secret formula to become a great writer. There is! I don't know all the elements, but establishing a routine, a habit, will have you emulating those who *are* successful. Ray Bradbury says to write a short story every week for a year, as it is virtually impossible to write that many stories and not have at least one good one. My own experience was to create a fishing metaphor: If I got up at four each morning, and chummed the waters, by 6:00 (the time I had to put everything on hold to get my kids to school) I would catch *something*.

The consensus is ... commit to a routine. This is what R.E. Harrington was really saying, even if it is to just 15 minutes a day. This is also what Pulitzer Prize-winner Bernard Malamud advocates:

> "You write by sitting down and writing. There's no particular time or place—you suit yourself, your nature .... Eventually everyone learns his or her own best way."

But here is a word of caution from E.B. White:

> "A writer who waits for ideal conditions under which to work will die without putting a word on paper."

Writer's Block is completely illusionary; it is procrastination masquerading as something noble. If this myth still holds power over you, if it is the dragon you are too timid to slay, consider the words of Ferdinand Foch, the prevailing French general of World War I:

> "The most powerful weapon on earth is the human spirit on fire."

Bet he had fire in the belly.

LESSON 6:

Sage Advice

WORKOUT

Assignment: You'll recall from the *Prelude to Performance* workout Milan Kundera's observation that a novel gives us a chance to experiment with invented personas we can assume for ourselves. In this exercise, assume that you are an editor, and have been one for perhaps the last 150 years, or, at least, if that sounds a bit hyperbolic, a good part of your adult life. What advice would *you* give to someone just starting out, thinking they have a story to tell? Half a page only.

Here's a reminder: I will reply with industrial-grade depth to this workout assignment and any or all assignments that follow each lesson if you are among those who have signed up for my Interactive Course.

https://gumroad.com/l/IPaVR

The entire tuition is deductible should you purchase a 20-hour block of time from services and fees you'll find listed at the end of the book, and you'll be entitled as well to a 10% discount on all other editing/ publishing plans.

LESSON 7:

Let's Make a Scene

Plot vs Premise/Scene vs Situation

You are a carpenter when you subject slabs of wood to your will, persuading them to behave to build something utilitarian, and you are (under)*paid* for your efforts. You are a plumber when you are *paid* to clear the capillaries of congested pipes or do a bypass to assert your dominion over the flow of water and perhaps, effluent for the affluent. Often a wrenching experience. And you are a dentist when, after extensive schooling, you drill, fill and bill.

But when can you call yourself a writer? When you are first published? When the first royalty checks floating in? When you can quit the day job? You are a writer if you *write. Period.* Or, better still, exclamation point! Step number one is not just to tell yourself that, but everyone who asks "What do you do?"

(We'll work that into a writing exercise in this session.)

Stephen King was working in a Laundromat when he picked up the phone in the days before caller-id. After he hung up the phone—(Millennials, in pre-cell phone days, a call was terminated by physically replacing the phone on a receiver, either on a desk or hanging on a wall—thought you'd like to know!) and made a call himself, to his wife, Tabitha, saying "The next thing I launder will be money." He had just sold *Carrie* (actually, the manuscript—Carrie was his fictitious person) for $400,000. (OK. Maybe he didn't say that, but my poetic license is good till my birthday in 2024. The rights to the paperback *did* sell for **$2,567,091.36** in today's dollars). Tabitha, by the way, had pulled *Carrie* out of the trash bin and made Stephen finish it.

But Stephen King was a writer before the sale, the day he picked up a pen.

In a second of "By-the-ways" by the way, you don't have to stand in line at the DMV to get a poetic license. Don't even need a photo ID. Richard Nixon (in)famously said, "If the President of the United States does it, it's not illegal." If a properly poetically licensed writer makes preposterous claims, it's not illegal. Reminding you of Chief Bromden's declaration in the first pages of *One Flew Over the Cuckoo's Nest*, "It's the truth, even if it didn't happen."

Pop quiz! Are you a writer? (That's not a trick question!)

In a moment I'm going to ask you to rewrite a scene. A *scene* is the dramatic core of a novel, it advances plot and characterization—one or the other or both. It's the *place* where something happens. A scene does not materialize from nowhere: it is birthed by a *situation*, the set of circumstances that encapsulate your character. "Their mutual infidelity was intolerable,"—the *situation*. "They could work it out in the bedroom or the courtroom,"—either place would be the scene.

A *situation* engages the mind; a scene massages the *senses*. Any scene you write must appeal to the senses. BTW#3: If you are a writer, you're *supposed* to be sensitive; it's part of the job description, but most people misuse or misunderstand the word. Take it at face value; if you're sensitive, you *sense* things, either intuiting something intangible, like the motives behind your character's shyness or audacity before something occurs to substantiate it, or something physical, like sensing the wind, smelling the chocolate, tasting the salt. Often, being sensitive is an accusation, meaning easily hurt. If someone says you're too sensitive, they ain't talking about the receptors on the tip of your tongue, but how easily your psyche bruises.

So, go ahead; be sensitive. Caffeinate all your senses when you write a scene. What does the room taste, smell, feel like? What is it that the fire in the hearth does to the room? To the characters in the room? How does the wine taste? How does your mouth feel as you sip or swallow? What does her voice sound like, and how can you use that description to define her or move the plot? A husky, cigarette-damaged voice? The voice of a wounded animal? A seductress? An innocent? Fearful? Brave? Engage all your senses and use them to create the scene. Embellish: you can (and should) come back later and delete what is extraneous, but for now, the potter's wheel needs clay. Why is that scent of cologne so offensive? Use your senses not only for descriptions, but to pace dialogue and create nuance in speech and speech patterns. What is it you *sense* by the gravel in his voice? Why did he hesitate so long before answering?

Here is some supportive advice from Ernest Hemingway, who has just escorted your character into the room:

"When people talk, listen completely. Don't be thinking what you're going to say. Most people never listen. Nor do they observe. You should be able to go into a room and when you come out know everything that you saw there and not only that. If that room gave you any feeling you should know exactly what it was that gave you that feeling."

Of course, if you are thinking what you'll say, it is at the expense of spontaneity, the Holy Grail of dialogue.

OK. I've chummed the waters with a few lines for a scene I ask you now to read and then rewrite, based on this situation: You (or your character) has decided not to be defensive anymore by asserting that you/he/she is a writer, even though never published. The scene is a dinner party. Make your choices. Formal? Casual? Intermission at the Opera? Backyard barbeque? What are you drinking? The banter begins, and the moment after the stranger asks your name, comes the standard question. What are you going to tell him?

"So ... what do you do?"

"I write."

"Oh? Anything I might have read?"

"Not likely. I have never been published." (though it is more accurate to say "I have not yet been published.")

Your stranger was expecting an answer like "I am a carpenter/plumber/dentist." How you are connected *financially* to the world.

But you have really told him how you *are* connected to the world. You have told him how you make a life, not a living. You have told him who you are, not what you do, leaving him a bit perplexed that your declarative statement did not end with a $ sign, but instead with a period, or exclamation point! You are now in a liberated stage of the conversation. It is absolutely glorious to acknowledge, without apology, that you are a writer.

"That's right. I'm a writer. You gotta problem with that?"

Expand this scene yourself and see how to develop a dialogue between yourself and the stranger, considering these two opposing approaches to writing a novel:

One is to have a plot in mind before you write. A plot presupposes that you have an outcome firmly established. You have events sequenced in your head, maybe even on paper in outline form, each episode the basis for a chapter. After a reasonable number of chapters, your outcome, known all along to you but hopefully not telegraphed to your reader, will be revealed. To my thinking, a novel is not a term paper.

The other approach is to have a premise. Here is an example: Two strangers meet at a dinner party and after a polite introduction, a conversation begins that is surprising to one but not the other. When stranger number one asks, "What do you do?" he was expecting an answer something like. "I am a carpenter," which then allows him to reply what *he* does or make some comments about carpentry. Dull stuff. Maybe he's a little embarrassed for stranger number two, since everyone else in the room gets a pay-check from Merrill Lynch. Or maybe he's envious *because* everyone else in the room gets a pay-check from Merrill Lynch.

But you (or your character) have told him unapologetically that you are a writer.

A *plot* (think about that word—points on a two-dimensional graph, flat) is you or your client's preconceived plan of what will happen at this gathering. The two guests meet; one blandly/proudly/unassumingly reveals he is an investment banker. You've penciled in that his trophy wife sees that you have come unattached. Later in the evening you wander out on the balcony where she leans on the balustrade and, being a bit tipsy, she starts making confessions to you; she's later gonna regret it, and the behavior you intentionally foreshadow in the scene. You've got it all worked out. Foreshadowing in for play. Or foreplay!

With a *premise*, it is enough that two strangers meet at the party, one reveals that he is an investment banker/or writer, and then see what happens. Let your *characters* tell your readers what happens next. *You only have to put words in their mouths once.* "So … what do you do?" "I'm a writer." And they will take it from there. Trust them. You pulled them out of your own belly, didn't you? A premise *can* take you to the exact spot that a plot will! You *could* find yourself on the balcony with a vulnerable woman, but by letting the characters take you there, rather than having it a pre-ordained *plotted* occurrence, you get spontaneity, and you might have an outcome you didn't imagine when trying to invent a plot

that you thought would hold a reader's attention. Endless possibilities to launch a novel from this scene.

(BTW#4: a successful writer will rewrite his same first page 100 times—no hyperbole here, *really*—to create the illusion of spontaneity. Call it re-*righting*.) And here's a thought; how about writing the same scene you just penned but from the point of view of the wife?

Am I holding your attention here? I started this musing with a premise, not a plot, and as a result I am now going into turf I didn't expect to cover here. Plotting would have thwarted that. My *premise* was to talk about being a carpenter, and show how it is analogous to being a writer. I was, in fact, an accomplished finish carpenter (now there's an oxymoron: a carpenter who finishes!) before I came out as a writer. And I could not totally enjoy the experience of eating in an elegant restaurant replete with highly varnished black walnut wainscoting and crown moldings because I was picking it apart. How tight are the joints? Are the finish nails embedded where there are naturally occurring knots in the wood, the better to hide them? Do the grains in one panel bear a relationship, a consideration or harmony to the panels to its left and right?

Anyone else joining me for dinner would have had the pleasure, the totality of the visual experience and sense of elegance without diminishing it by being analytical.

And so, the point to the analogy: If you over-study the art/craft of writing, you can miss the totality of the experience, of the pleasure of delving into a good book. University English touts the value of "close reading." Why did Nobel Laureate Bob Dylan write "My love is like *some* raven, at my window with a broken wing?" Why not "… like a raven?" The first two-and-a-half hours in an upper division English class devoted to Cormac McCarthy was spent divining the intent of the first sentence in *Blood Meridian*, "See the child." I saw the child.

Fortunately for me, the first time I read *The Old Man and the Sea* I was only 10 or 12 years old, and I have probably read it a half a dozen times more in my lifetime (and will read it again). On the first page, "The sail was patched with flour sacks and, furled, it looked like the flag of permanent defeat." Did I really need to know that "like the flag of permanent defeat" was a simile? Or that, if restated "it was the flag of permanent defeat" would have made it a metaphor?

Within the first paragraph, a mood is set. I'm in. I was in before anything I knew about the author contaminated the experience of reading the story.

Ernest who? I was too young at the first reading to grasp what humility was, but even as a pre-teen I could feel sadness for an impoverished old man who was not made for defeat.

If you agree you should not be analytical when you read, then neither should you be self-analytical as you write your first drafts.

> "I do not over–intellectualize the production process. I try to keep it simple: Tell the damned story."

> Tom Clancy

And yet, hypocrite that I am, I want to impart upon you, or at least, offer, observations that will make you a better writer.

There are at least 30 literary devices; that is, knowable, defined implementations that enhance your ability to achieve your goal: addicting your reader to turning pages. Reading back on this chapter, I hi-lighted at least 50% of these devices that make the read more compelling for you. Simile, metaphor, personification, satire, sarcasm, oxymoron, euphemism, consonance, epigraph, repetition, double-entendre, anthropomorphism, allegory, anaphora, alliteration, colloquialism, malapropism, hyperbole, and …?

Did you really need to know that all of those literary devices crept in there? And what literary device is it that these abstract concepts "creep" in there? And isn't it more engaging that they creep in there, rather than stating "these literary devices are located within the preceding text?"

The trail of literary devices in this chapter begins at the beginning, with a double entendre' an alliterating subtitle!

Let's Make a Scene
Plot vs Premise/Scene vs Situation

And it just doesn't let up. Did I miss any?

"persuading them to behave"
personification
giving the planks human qualities, to wit; the capacity to behave or misbehave
(Personification occurs when an inanimate object or nonhuman figure is embodied with human-like qualities or characteristics. This contrasts with *anthropomorphism*, in which non-human figures actually become human-like characters, rather than just being described as having human-like traits. That serpent handing out apples in the Garden of Eden? Anthropomorphic.)

"(under)*paid*"
sarcasm
As a former carpenter I recall inviting my long-time friend Jimmy Joyce to fly over from the UK to work with me on a project I ran in La Jolla. After strapping on his "pockets" (the belt that holds nails and tools) he informed me and the rest of the crew, "All right. There're only two topics of conversation on this site: women and we ain't gettin' paid enough."

"clear the capillaries of congested pipes"
alliteration
clear, capillaries/congested, and personification as well, ascribing human traits to pipes

"do a bypass"
a metaphorical expression for re-routing pipes, and, once again, personification because a by-pass is a surgical procedure performed on humans

"assert your dominion over the flow of water and perhaps, effluent for the affluent"
personification, alliteration
Since *asserting your dominium* is associated with power over man and beast, you have personified *water* and *effluent* by implication. Also at play alliteration, and consonance, the sounds of the words *effluent* and *affluent* being alliteration by virtue of similar beginnings of *ef* and *af*, and consonance by the totality of the words.

"often a wrenching experience"
double entendre, and sarcasm

"you drill, fill and *bill*"
consonance—sounds in harmony—and sarcasm

"when you can quit the day job"
a metaphorical way of saying that he was at last a success, symbolized by being able to abandon the necessity to work at a menial job for survival

"when he picked up the phone"
a metaphorical way of saying he was informed

"The next thing I launder will be money."
double entendre, sarcasm

"Tabitha […] pulled *Carrie* out of the trash bin and made Stephen finish it.
metaphorical *action*, personification
While Tabitha may literally have "pulled" Carrie from the trash bin, in all likelihood she was really just persuading her husband to continue with a project he had discarded. And "Carrie" is an inanimate object, a manuscript, now referred to as human. Personification, and the case could be made that it's anthropomorphic.

"picked up a pen"
the traditional metaphorical way of saying "he became a writer," or "started writing"

"it's part of the job description"
a colloquialism, a metaphorical way of saying *it's what's expected of you*

"the Holy Grail of dialogue"
hyperbole, metaphor amplifying the importance of dialogue in the ranking of all things a writer must consider

"I've chummed the waters"
colloquialism based on the fishing metaphor as the technique to lure fish within range

"telegraphed"
colloquialism, metaphor

"everyone else in the room gets a paycheck from Merrill Lynch"
hyperbole, metaphor
Probably no one even works for Merrill Lynch. Some of the attendees may not work at all. Metaphor. Those who are employed using their intellect as opposed to physical labor, or those employed in the cranial financial sector. everyone else in the room gets a paycheck from Merrill Lynch. The sentences in tandem demonstrate sarcasm, irony. A finer point: though the sentences are repetitive, I would not say that this is an example of *repetition* as a literary device. Repetition is used to drive home the same point; it's about emphasis. Repetition here is in the service of sarcasm.

"you've penciled in"
colloquialism, verbal metaphor

"trophy wife"
a (rather demeaning) metaphor. Objectifying rather than personifying

"being a bit tipsy"
colloquialism, metaphor

"gonna"
colloquialism

"Foreshadowing in for play. Or foreplay!"
alliteration, double-entendre

"re-*righting*"
malapropism
Let me save you the trouble of looking it up in Webster's:
"an act or habit of misusing words ridiculously, especially by the confusion of words that are similar in sound."

"finish carpenter: a carpenter who finishes"
double-entendre (triple if the carpenter is from Helsinki) Sarcastic oxymoron
Ever hired a carpenter who actually *finished* the job?

"I came out as a writer"
colloquialism, an evolved expression that has come to mean acknowledging something you may have at one time been reluctant to admit

"the totality of the visual experience/the totality of the experience"
repetition

"it looked like the flag of permanent defeat"
simile

"it was the flag of permanent defeat"
metaphor

"I'm in"
colloquialism for enthused

Fortunately, most of the expressions I used are common enough in speech that they can easily slip into the text without much fanfare. In the best-case scenario, you may not even be aware that you are using literary devices. Though a writer's stock-and-trade is imagination, can you imagine Hemingway saying to himself, "I think I need a simile to describe the sad-looking sail, patched with a flour sack?" I think instead he just saw in his mind's eye, that, unfurled, it looked like the permanent flag of defeat.

LESSON 7:

Let's make a Scene

WORKOUT

Assignment: This is a two-parter.

First, Plot vs Premise: You plan to rob a bank. Plot it out and write the first two paragraphs entering the bank. Or take the premise route: Your protagonist has lost all income due to a pandemic raging across the country and has a wife and infant to feed. All possibilities for honest money have evaporated. What does he think? What does he do? Two paragraphs.

Part two: Scene vs Situation. This one's easy. Pull up on Turner Classics or Netflix *To Kill a Mockingbird*. The *situation* is that Tom Robbins' life is at stake; the *scene* is the courtroom where Atticus Finch must save his life. The scene is also a good example of *bookending* discussed in our final lesson. We begin with Scout, the daughter of Atticus, wiggling her way into the upper gallery of the courtroom to watch the proceedings. We *bookend* with Atticus, oblivious to being witnessed by the rapt audience above him, making his exit, as a black man prods Scout, "Stand up. Your Father's passing."

LESSON 8:

Writers' Beat-Ups

"Unless a critic is prepared to give unmitigated praise, I say, to hell with the bastard."

John Steinbeck

Can you even imagine Ernest Hemingway attending a writer's workshop or meet-up?

"Hi, what's your name?"

"Ernest. But a lotta people call me Papa."

"Well, then, welcome Papa. And what have you brought to share with the group tonight?"

"Well, I have a story about fishing."

"A how-to?"

"No. It's about this fisherman who has all these thoughts while he's out trying to land the big one."

"Not much a plot there, Papa, I mean he goes fishing. Anything else happen?"

"No. That's about it."

"Well, thank you for coming. Would anyone like to comment on Papa's idea? You, Judy?"

"Yes. Papa, you'll need a plot with a bit more of a hook! Oh! Ha-ha, a *hook*. But all jocularity aside, you need to have conflict to drive your novel. Are there zombies?"

"No, but, well, after he catches a big marlin, sharks come and eat it before he can make it back to the harbor."

"Why doesn't he just winch the thing up on board?"

"It's a small boat. Just a skiff, actually. He's very poor, and its only power is a small sail, which, unfurled, looks like the flag of permanent defeat. So it takes him a while to get back home."

"That's really sad. You need to give your readers something more uplifting. Ha-ha, there I go again! A winch? Uplifting? But seriously, think about it."

I can recall a writers' workshop I hosted, attended by about 15 mostly fledgling writers, though a couple among them had been published—one fiction, one non-fiction. There was a new guy in attendance, Tom, who had wandered into my office in the early afternoon before the evening's meet-up, and we shot the excrement for a while and I got to know a bit about his background. Most impressive!

Our meet-up got underway. As usual I made it a point to just fill the coffee cups and let someone else actually conduct the meeting, only interceding if things got nasty. The formula was that you read two or three pages, and you had printed copies that you gave to each attendee, so they could make notes to hand back to you at the end of the meeting. (Sound familiar?) On this particular evening, Ron, our published non-fiction writer, held the imaginary conch shell. Like the savage little boys in *Lord of the Flies,* you could only speak if you held the shell.

For some unknown reason, writers in meetups introduce themselves only by their first names, like an AA meeting. Ron looked to see who was shuffling papers, a sure sign they were hoping to "share" next. The only one not shuffling papers was wedged in between two of the regulars, Tom. Was he shy? Didn't know the protocols?

"Tom, welcome. Did you bring something you'd like to read?"

"Sure, Ron. Thanks. Let me give you the set-up before I ...."

"No, no, no, Tom. It's better to just read rather than trying to explain yourself. You'll see."

"As you like," he shrugged, and then read the start of a story of an American in a small village in France who goes into a boulangerie to buy a baguette. He does not speak French, and the two young women behind the counter know this and are free to gossip about him. When he pays for the bread and assorted pastries, he leaves five euros instead of the 3.50 that it actually costs. The women call him arrogant. Tom's writing gives explanations for the actions of his protagonist, and the actions of the two behind the counter.

When Tom has finished. Ron tells him, "You need to show, don't tell."

The table of critics nod in agreement. Yeah, show don't tell.

"Actually, I'm pretty happy with it as it stands."

Judy, the published fiction writer, chimes in. "Ron is right. Your writing will be much more effective if you *show* he is arrogant, rather than having the girls behind the counter *telling* you he's arrogant."

Heads continue to bob up and down, with sympathetic glances to the new guy.

"Honestly, I am quite happy with how it all unfolds."

"You shouldn't be defensive," said Ron, putting Tom on the defensive. "We are here to help you. Listen to Judy. She's a professional writer."

I can see it coming.

"Are you a professional writer?" asks Ron, sure he knows the answer.

And without a hint of arrogance that his baguette-buying protagonist has, Tom answers, "Yes. Actually, I am. I write for the *Chicago Sun*, and although I've never gotten it, I've been nominated four times for a Pulitzer."

You coulda heard a *sin* drop.

The point is, *you* are the world's leading authority on your story, AND the style by which you choose to tell it. It either works, or it doesn't. And don't worry if you break some of the conventional rules you've recently discovered in Writing 101, because James Joyce already broke all those rules for you.

It has been my experience, through 150! meetups and writers' workshops, that EVERYONE feels compelled to offer an opinion on your work. If the iron ore in your blood can't resist the magnetic pull of a writers' group, here's a few suggestions.

Editor-in-Chief leading a writers' workshop in search of a coffee shop. © Thornton Sully

81

Consider the likelihood that you will be evaluated by amateurs. Perhaps well-intentioned, but amateurs, nonetheless. Understand the difference between *advice* and *feedback*. Advice for Tom might be the cliché "show, don't tell." But feedback is much more valuable, nuanced: "I did not feel any emotional interplay between the Yank and the French girl in the boulangerie." This actually was what Tom had intended; his character is emotionally closed, and as the story develops, an affair with the French girl brings him to realize his stoicism as a defect, depriving him of the pleasure of being in France, alive, and on the planet. If Tom had wanted there to be some sort of emotional spark in the encounter, your comment then, your *feedback* that you didn't feel it, without telling him how to fix may be just what he needed, and what he came to hear from the group.

You might also try having someone else read your work aloud to the group rather than doing it yourself. Try to pick someone of the same gender, and if possible, the same approximate age and circumstances. This opens up possibilities: First, hearing your own words spoken by others will immediately alert you to things you want to edit that don't show necessarily when you are working with written text. Secondly, while they are reading your words, YOU are reading body language. How are people responding to what is being read? Do they look bored? Do their eyes wander? Do they whisper unrelated conversations to someone sitting next to them, or are they, literally, hanging on the edge of their seat, hanging on to every word?

Why did you attend this group? The politically correct answer is "to have my work critiqued and become a better writer." Nevertheless, it's fine if your motivation is simply to drink wine/coffee/tea/cognac in the company of creative people, without an obligation to produce a better manuscript. In fact, with that sort of relaxed attitude, paradoxically you may find your work improving, by however you care to measure it.

I also believe, and perhaps it comes from so much time spent in both Chinese and Malay culture, that no negative criticism whatsoever should be given in a group setting. If someone gives you the privilege of reading their writing, or they read it to you out loud, tell them your thoughts privately if you risk discouraging them.

"Mi hijito, I've told you a thousand times, if you speak badly of people, God will punish you and make you just like them."

Victor Villaseñor, *Rain of Gold*

To which Hemingway adds:

> "I like to listen. I have learned a great deal from listening carefully. Most people never listen."

So, if I can't give "constructive criticism," the ultimate oxymoron, how can I help, how can you help, a writer to become more competent and more sure of themselves? Hang with me for a minute. Here's an appearance from Mark Twain. (You'll see this worth-repeating quote again.)

> "Whenever you see an adjective, kill it."

John Adams was notoriously known for his fealty to adjectives. "Why use a single adjective when six are for hire?" was his reasoning. Just for fun, write a sentence describing the coffee cup fueling your present bout with the quill and parchment. Wrapping your adjectives around the cup will not cause it to hold more coffee, insulate your fingers from the heat, or advance your story.

And yet, adjectives are the apron strings that tie a writer to Mrs. Marabel's freshman English class, the one where you pumped up your sentences to fill the page to meet the length requirements of the mid-term essay. Do as mercenary Mark Twain did. A novel is nouns and verbs. Use glorious, inspiring, clarifying, important, necessary, compelling, essential, edifying, complicated, simplifying, memorable … intriguing … unforgettable … (blah blah blah) *adjectives* (*and adverbs*) sparingly.

Nevertheless, I have rarely met a fledgling writer who did not have an addictive love affair with his adjectives with a serenade on every page. (Hark! What light through yonder translucent, double-paned, unwashed balcony window breaks?) This is problematic in a writers' meet-up group, because others in the group may have gotten ahead of the new guy to chapter three in their *how-to* manual and know that adjectives need to be curtailed.

This has happened with enough frequency that it bears drawing attention to it: A writer brings in his three pages. Paragraph one, true to form, has more adjectives than I have personal defects, and he begins to read. Upon completion of his reading, the guillotine builds momentum.

"You've got way too many adjectives in your first paragraph, dude." A few variations of the same comment from others.

So, what if it's true? All the writer learns is that their effort is unappreciated and unworthy.

But look. That writer is there by intent. They want to write, and they want to do it well.

So, here is how I help: I will read through the first paragraph or page, the second, the third, and eventually I will find a well-constructed, compelling paragraph. THAT is the time to comment.

"You know, I really like this paragraph. It's succinct, and it shows you intuitively know that a novel is primarily nouns and verbs. This demonstrates that very well, and the very few adjectives you have chosen are well placed, and appropriate to keep the story moving. Well done."

No mention of the first paragraph. AND! A writer, and in my experience, particularly a new writer, very much wants approval for their efforts. (And why not?) They will see what received praise and replicate that in his future writing. They may eventually go back to their original first paragraph, see it bursting with adjectives, and wonder how they ever came to do that.

If you are a decent person, you will not willfully hurt a fellow being with criticism, especially since writers tend to be more easily bruised than others. But there is a pragmatic reason for being kind to someone whose work is (to yours or collective, subjective judgment) mediocre, or someone whose writing is so bad you want to edit it first before throwing it away. *Somebody* is going to surprise you.

Allen was a regular at a weekly writers' workshop I held in Oceanside. Each week, everyone listened politely as he read his story, sometimes the same story as the week before but with a word or two changed here and there. We knew what to expect. We would recycle some of the same comments from the week before, maybe even forgetting they were recycled. His stuff was just boring, painfully so. But then one evening, when Allen read something new he had been working on, magic happened. He hit his stride. He was brilliant. His *work* was brilliant, energized. I don't know how that happens, especially such a quick transformation. What would have happened if we had discouraged him with negativity?

A brief explanation of how *A Word with You Press* came into being to give context to what I would like to impart: I completed a novel, *The Boy with a Torn Hat* in 2009 to coincide (not by plan!) with a recession that prompted Random House to lay off a hundred people. With such a bare-bones staff, it seemed highly unlikely that my novel would get much attention, even if they picked it up. I decided I would publish it myself, and I created a website to showcase it. People would visit the website, read a sampling, fall in love with the story and click "buy." Easy-Peasy. But people don't just stumble onto a website, so I advertised a contest on Craigslist with a promise to publish the best 100 stories submitted. Write a page about anything at all but tie it back to a cup of coffee. 500 queries and 150 entries later, we published *The Coffeeshop Chronicles: Oh, The Places I have Bean!*

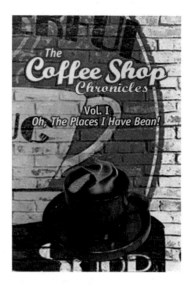

The contest needed a winner. One of the earlier entries I almost declined to post, as it started out with its character masturbating while staring at the ceiling listening to the love making from the upstairs neighbors. It seemed gratuitously pornographic. And it started with a profanity.

I decided to reply to his entry, and I made a mild suggestion that if he wanted to use profanity, postpone it until he had established a rapport with his readers, as some might be put off with an immediate use of profanity. (I have no problem with profanity, but it must be wielded prudishly—OOPS! PRUDENTLY!) Surprising me, he followed my advice, and resubmitted his story. We went back and forth three more times, and it became clear to me that this was a writer seriously interested in telling a story and asking for guidance. A story that at first read seemed to be about a frustrated stalker revealed itself to be a story of unfulfilled longing, that used metaphor and rhythm and imagery to great effect. He put his heart on his sleeve. Are you willing to do the same when you write, even if you disguise it behind a fictitious character, your "experimental self" as Milan Kundera would say? I hope that I never again underestimate a writer's ability to exceed my expectations, and I encourage you, if you are getting some value from attending writer meetups, to allow yourself to be amazed at how the act of writing, done repetitively and with diligence, can uncover your own greatness and that of your fellow storytellers. Restraining my initial impulse to sink a writer's first attempts into the bin was rewarded with *My Day Off.*

LESSON 8:

Writers' Beat-Ups

WORKOUT

Assignment: Here's an easy one. Attend a writers' workshop, and, before you go, commit to volunteering absolutely no opinion or comments on anyone's writing.

> "As a writer, you should not judge, you should understand."
>
> Ernest Hemingway

Here's a concurring opinion:

> "The beginning of all wisdom is to understand that you don't know. To know is the enemy of all learning. To be sure is the enemy of wisdom."
>
> Victor Villaseñor,
> *Burro Genius*

Here's a special invitation:
Send an email to me at thorn@awordwithyoupress.com if you'd like me to Zoom in on your writer's group of six or more to speak of any subject of your choice regarding publishing, editing, or writing. Together we'll choose a topic and arrange a time.

LESSON 9:

Credible Critiques

It is important that if you compliment a writer, especially a novice, for a job well done, you can articulate the reasons you say the work is good. False flattery ultimately fails. Most people know if you're blowing smoke up their exit portal. If you say, "This is really good," be prepared to say why. Be prepared to fill in the blanks with something meaningful that says more than just that the story appeals to your subjective tastes. Multiple times I have been presented with manuscripts to edit or publish by a writer who is convinced it needs no editing, because his circle of readers, either friends or co-conspirators in a writing group have said "I really like it" or lob a few superlatives in his direction. If you begin with "I really like this," though you were well intentioned to provide encouragement, your effort is undermined without a supporting evidentiary explanation.

My Day Off ... This is really good. I really like this because ... well ... read the story and I'll tell you, in my both my subjective but professional opinion, why it's really good, and why I really like it.

———

MY DAY OFF

By Juan Vandendorp

The Parisian subway train tore along the tunnel with a clumsy rhythm. I took my eyes away from the window and leaned back against the upholstered seat; I glanced around the half empty car at the sad looking passengers. When we pulled in the station, I looked across the platform at a homeless man sound asleep on a bench, under a gigantic poster of a Simmons mattress. It was then, when the doors slid shut and the train peered deep into the dark tunnel ahead, that I saw the woman. She stood by the door, reading a paperback that she held at eye level; her slim body rocked slightly to the movement of the train, her left hand clutched the overhead rail. My body started shaking inexplicably, against my will. I felt as if I had done something terribly wrong and was ashamed. My breathing became agitated and I gasped for air; were people looking at me? I forced my body to behave, and, positive that she could not see me, I explored her.

Her skin was white, baby-like, and had a film of blond hair only I could notice. Her pale, blue eyes followed the pages with intent, oblivious to the world. I watched the woman's Yves St. Laurent navy two-piece reflected in the window glass; I straightened my shirt collar and tried to hand-iron my pants without success; I wiped my bald head with my hand and wished it didn't look like a freeway. She reminded me of a young Charlotte Rampling, with her sad blue eyes and her graceful movements. She got off at *Montparnasse*, which was not my stop, but I got up and started following her; I realized I had never followed anyone before. The cobblestones in the street were wet and dirty and the smell of urine rose from the gutter; she walked twenty meters ahead of me, a white rose in a charred battlefield.

She sat at a terrace and said to the waiter: *"Un café, s'il vous plait."* I went to the bar and ordered a coffee. I sipped it as I tried to see which book she was reading. The waiter noticed that I was staring at the woman and smiled at me. I was embarrassed at my transparency, but my remote hope of meeting this woman was stronger than my shame. I stayed put. After one hour, the woman got up and headed for the metro entrance at *Montparnasse*; I started after her, feeling a bit edgy from that strong Parisian coffee. She went into a book shop at *la rue Duret* and I paced outside, entertaining possible scenarios to approach her. A handsome young man went by and I wished I could have snatched his body for a minute. I was thinking of James Bond when the woman stepped out, walked a few meters and sat at yet another terrace with a red awning and waiters wearing white aprons over black pants. *Paris and these over-caffeinated Parisians,* I thought. *"Et pour Monsieur?"* I heard a half-whispered voice behind me. I was startled, and reflexively told the waiter, *"Un espresso."* The woman had bought a book by Jorge Luis Borges that I happened to know; my chest beat hard as some part of me plotted to sit at her table; the sound of the steaming demitasse the waiter delivered upon the table made the sharp ping of a judge's gavel, sentencing me to remain still. The woman found the book fascinating for she read forever and had three more cups of coffee; I kept up with the caffeine intake and by now I was shaking like a snare drum and kept switching positions in my chair.

But this is battle, I thought, *this is war*; my bladder would have to wait and losing my kidneys was a small price to pay to be in a cosmic scene with her. She kept reading in the metro and got off at *Bir Hakeim*, followed by a group of Japanese teenagers with dangling cameras. She walked along the deserted banks of the Seine toward the Eiffel Tower. *This is it,* I thought. My heart beat fast; I hurried down the stairs and there she was, strolling past a wooden bench with the Eiffel Tower in the background. I got close to her but when I was ten feet away all I could do was stop, terrified that she would turn around and see me. My heart wanted out of my chest, my legs shook. I stopped and saw her blond hair against the navy blue jacket become smaller and smaller. She climbed the stairs to the *Avenue de Suffren* and I watched her leave my life; a sailboat on the Seine caught my eye and I thought that I had never seen one before.

That night the five espressos kept me awake; I started imagining the two of us together. I stared at the humidity stain on the ceiling for a long time and listened to the moaning coming from my neighbor's apartment.

———

First, the reasons *it's good*, to be followed by the subjective reasons that *I really like it*:
1) *Clumsy* and *rhythm* catch my imagination, because the two terms create a tension between themselves. Rhythm generally applies something orderly. *Clumsy* contradicts that.
2) He personifies the train. It tears and peers. He uses personification and other literary devices seamlessly, and the personification adds to the human nature, the terribly human nature, of his sad narrative. The train

did not *move* along the tracks, it *tore* along the tunnel. The emotional content of the story is harsh. That tone is set by using an aggressive word such as *tore*. If the train *glided* along the tracks, or *slipped* through the tunnel, it would nullify the emotional rigors of his story. "[…] *tore* through the *tunnel*" is well-placed alliteration.

3) Another literary device, well placed and visually credible is the irony of seeing a homeless man asleep under a poster for a mattress. I wonder if it's a Simmons' Beauty-Rest?

4) He doesn't explain who Charlotte Rampling is. This to me demonstrates mature writing, because it doesn't even matter if we know who she is. It is enough to know it is someone intriguing or young and beautiful or all three of those things. The narrative would have been diminished if he explained to his readers who she is. (See info-dump.) What we know is the purpose she serves in his imagination.

5) The imagery is gorgeous: *The cobblestones in the street were wet and dirty and the smell of urine rose from the gutter; she walked twenty meters ahead of me, a white rose in a charred battlefield.*

Could Hemingway or Shakespeare have written more eloquently? Eloquence is the ability to say the most with the fewest number of words, and in this single passage, the author says so much not just for the scene at hand, the snippet of her walking away, but her alure is amplified by contrasting the pathetic condition of street and city. *Wet* and *dirty* pair together, enhanced by the smell of urine, the gutter, that amplify his perception of how absolutely lovely the woman is, the one completely oblivious to his existence or even presence.

6) *shaking like a snare drum* does everything a simile is capable of doing. Can't you just feel your own legs as he says that?

7) *The sound of the steaming demitasse the waiter delivered upon the table made the sharp ping of a judge's gavel, sentencing me to remain still.* A wonderful metaphor, and the gavel is personified, becoming the surrogate for a judge. (The gavel does not sentence him; the judge does.)

8) *she read forever* … is a perfect use of hyperbole as a literary device. It acknowledges his sense of frustration and that he has no agency here. And she is, throughout, completely oblivious to him.

9) Staring at the humidity stains on the ceiling for such a long time while subjected to the torture of hearing moaning which can only be the sounds of the lovemaking of the neighbors becomes a poignant metaphor of despair, of longing and of loneliness. A flag of permanent defeat.

It is difficult to defend the proposition that what is "good" writing is anything but subjective. I have tried to separate objective perceptions within *My Day Off* to justify my claim that it's a good piece of writing. What is easier, is for me to tell you why it resonated with me. I am telling you my set of values and prejudices; you certainly have your own.

Yes, I really liked the piece. Here's why:

I like that:
the writer does not try to make himself the hero of his own tale. He remembers that the story is always more important than the storyteller, in the same way that the song is always more important than the singer.

I like that:
the author demonstrates humility, one of mankind's finest virtues.

I like that:
the writer does not embellish an image of self, either with physical descriptions or by actions. "I wiped my hand over my bald head and wished it didn't look like a freeway."

I like that:

he avoided a Hollywood ending, where they do in fact meet and she is charmed.

I liked that:

I could feel his agony, expressed by staring at the stains on the ceiling, and listening to the passion on the other side of his bedroom wall that might have been his, had his self-image not been so small and damaged when he first saw the nameless woman.

I liked that:

I could have been this man. I have been this man, and I could be this man again. The writer's candor tells me that longing is not an anomaly or defect.

I like that:

the author makes no pretense of being an attractive male. Isn't a sense of being attractive something that swings on a pendulum, anyway?

I like that:

Juan shares what is authentic, not what he thinks is acceptable.

Offer me this kind of authenticity when you write. Offer this kind of authenticity to your readers. Flaws in presentation of a story can always be addressed, corrected, adjusted; that's why there are editors. But more than anything else, what an editor wants is authenticity. *My Day Off* gave me that.

LESSON 9:

Credible Critiques

WORKOUT

Assignment: Read a short story by a famous author. I would suggest *A Piece of Steak* by Jack London, who left the goldmines of Alaska with $4 worth of gold and a fortune in experiences. Read it without first having Wikipedia tell you what it's all about and why it's important, what its themes are, use of literary devices and so on. Write a one-page summary of how (or if) the story resonated with you. *Then* google the story to see what others have thought about it.

LESSON 10:

The Evolution of a Sentence

"When you find an adjective, kill it."

Mark Twain

If we can enhance the meaning of a sentence by changing a single word, our dependency on adjectives and adverbs diminishes. How can the changing of one word release us from our addiction to adjectives? Some words that are slight variations for the same action, event or object carry within them their own degree of intensity. Let's work with this sentence, pretending it is the lead-in for an essay or even just a declarative paragraph in which we will solicit donations from our readership:

The lack of funding is a barrier to the success of the project.

The adjectives we might choose to turn up the volume might make the sentence look like this:

The lack of funding is a severe/discouraging barrier to the success of the project.

Everybody knows what a barrier is; it's something that *passively* occupies space between you and what you desire. Could be a traffic cone, a caution tape declaring "crime scene," a paltry B+ average when applying to Harvard Law School, a pimple sprouting on your face the day you worked up the courage to ask her out on a date. But all these are pretty flaccid; *barrier* lacks octane.

While *barrier* is neutral (neutered), something inherently passive, *barricade* implies a back-story of *action*. The French Revolution! *Vive la France! Barricades* are all that stand between us and the *gendarmes* intent on slaughtering us. So now our lead-in sentence is:

The lack of funding is a barricade to the success of the project.

Barricade is a much more visceral metaphor, and far more potent and engaging than any number of adjectives we are tempted to apply to *barrier. Barricade! Life or death!* This first step in the evolution of our sentence signals to our readers they may be called into action, as they immediately understand a volley of their dollars might be the salvo of salvation.

Let's keep this evolving.

We're looking for a masterpiece sentence to seduce our reader into the bed of our story. "Lack of funding" is oestrogen/testosterone free, cranial. We cannot visualize "lack of," (though we know what it means) but we can visualize, even feel, *anaemic.*

> *Anaemic funding is a barricade to the success of the project.*

The next order of business is to get rid of "to be" verbs. "Is" does not show action, but rather, like *am/are/was/were*, tells us about a state of being. Pablum, apple sauce, when what our carnivorous readers want is steak. To be? Or not to be? Not to be. We've invested our powers of intellect and creativity to morph "barriers" into "barricades," but now it may time to murder the little darlings, an editor's shorthand for deleting your favorite words if they don't serve the higher purpose of your intent, which is for your lead sentence to convey to the reader that the project is at risk because it

Bill Sikes

can't meet the payroll or electric bill or bar tab, and that something must be done about it. Maybe we *don't* need to choose between *barricade* and *barrier* to indicate urgency. Maybe there's another way. Keep exploring.

> *Anaemic funding starves the project?*

Maybe.

As you experiment with different words, do keep it in the

present tense. This is not a post-mortem. It is soon to become a call to arms. When we infused the inanimate construct *funding* with anaemia, we *personified* it. Now, in human form, its face is gaunt, and its drinking buddy is the Grim Reaper. That villainous *Anaemic funding* is *Oliver Twist's* Bill Sikes, with the capacity, the power, to collapse, suffocate, kill, murder or maim the project in which your dreams are invested. In its/his grip, a gnarled shillelagh.

> *Anaemic funding is bludgeoning the success of the project.*

> *Anaemic funding bludgeons the success of the project.*

In your opinion, does the word "is" contribute to the strength or understanding of the sentence? Here the response could be a bit more nuanced. Although we're talking about a "to be" verb that I just disparaged, in this instance because it implies something that is ongoing, I opt for keeping the word "is" in the text. But we still can do more to pump up the adrenals.

Do we lose anything if we delete reference to "success?" I think not.

> *Anaemic funding is bludgeoning the project.*

"Success" is implied. Unnecessary verbiage takes up too much space on paper and in your head.

Now, a final possibility, knowing that nothing is *really* final until it appears in print: What more can we do to predispose our reader to action before they read any further? Salute the flag? Or salute *our* flag. Join the family? Or join *our* family. Pointing out these kinds of subtleties to your client will inspire them to mention you when they accept their Pulitzer, because they can apply this principle not just to this single sentence, but to their future text. A good exercise for you to suggest would be to have them take a look at their own work, written but not scrutinized, to see if they can turn bland articles of speech into possessive pronouns. Change "the" to "our."

We now end up with a lead sentence that pecks through its shell:

> *The lack of funding is a barrier to the success of the project.*

to one that has found its wings:

Anaemic funding is bludgeoning our project.

By making that subtle change, you have just made every one of your readers a stakeholder.

———•———

WHAT'S FOR LUNCH?

Here's something else well worth considering as you retool your sentences ….

If I ask you what you had for lunch, and you answered "Food," you've answered the question, but told me nothing. If Erika, in your novel, sits down for lunch, the sentence is not *Erika sat down and had lunch*. Instead, *Erika signaled the waiter, having perused the menu and settled on the lobster bisque.* Or *It being Friday, Erika asked if sea bass was on the menu.* Or *Erika answered the rasping "Welcome to MacDonald's. How may I help you?" voice with "Number three combo, and super-size it."*

Unless it's the Last Supper, Erika simply sitting down to have lunch does nothing to advance your plot and misses a great opportunity to tell us something about the woman. Waiter? Lobster bisque? Perusing a menu rather than reading it or glancing at it? You know without me spelling it out what these clues imply, and so will your reader. Hmnn … What demographic would be concerned about eating fish on Friday? Though not completely defining a person with this single hint, what kind of person goes through a drive-thru and says "Super-size it?" Someone who at the very least has done this enough times to know what "super-size it" means. "I'll have the lobster bisque, and super-size it?"

Ian Fleming did not have James Bond sit at the bar and order a drink. He ordered a Vodka Martini, *Shaken. Not Stirred!*

Consider each time you make that evolutionary pass at your draft, it's a new generation of fledgling sentences, each one better suited for flight and survival than the one preceding it. Make Darwin proud!

LESSON 10:

The Evolution of a Sentence

WORKOUT

Assignment: Find three or more sentences in your own work that are in passive voice, and change them to active voice, in addition to this one:

It has been said that the road to Hell is paved with good intentions.

LESSON 11:

Your Turn

Wasn't it annoying in Driver's Ed to listen to classroom lectures when what you really wanted was to get behind the wheel? Get behind the wheel, now.

Write a brief story using the prompt:

The key broke off in the lock. He/she had to break through the door.

I would like your story, if possible, to use expansive language and metaphor, and maybe three literary devices, but it is not an absolute requirement. Just write whatever your muse directs you to do.

An *action* can also be metaphorical, as is the prompt to which you are writing. Our prompt could be a metaphor for determination: resistance overcome by willpower. It could also be viewed as a metaphor for assault or rape. It is an ambiguous prompt, which allows for your own interpretation.

Give yourself half an hour, while I have another cappuccino/rum-and-coke/shower/look at the personals/check my Paypal account, change the litter box, or whatever … but spoiler alert: I've already written something for this prompt, and will use it to demonstrate several literary principles when you return ….

… So, 30 minutes hence. I really hope you wrote something.

Here is what I came up with in response to the prompt:

The key broke off in the lock. He/she had to break through the door.

"No. No fucking way."

You risk alienating some of your readers if you start with profanity. If you avoid starting off with profanity, the trade-off is the loss of perceived authenticity of dialogue, but in my opinion, it is better to wait until you have established a rapport with your readers, and they like you before you use crass language. AND harsh language that is not standard profanity can also be authentic, dependent upon the character in your story. Remember, once you have reached for words like "motherfucker" you have nowhere left to go. Use profanity sparingly for the best effect. If I were to follow my own advice, I would have saved discussion that included profanities after I had gained your confidence by discussing less controversial elements of style. Was it awkward for you to read that first? Did you feel at all uncomfortable or put off by the language?

I also started my story with dialogue. (Right in the middle of a story, as opposed to setting the scene first.) And I do not start *ad ovum*—from the egg, which would have looked something like "the man enters the hallway and tries the lock, and when the key fails, breaks down the door."

"Just open the goddamn door."

Drama and conflict already established with an action and resistance. Do not use exclamation marks if the dialogue itself is exclamatory. The reader does not need that clue if the dialogue is strong.

Rachel gathered the evidence and stumbled to the bathroom to the beat of a man's heavy fist on a heavy door, pounding to the War of 1812.

Notice first the repetition of "heavy fist/heavy door." Do you think it sounds stronger than just "heavy fist on the door?" Don't identify what the evidence is; allow your reader the pleasure of speculating.

The sound of the woman/girl's name is harsh. The story is harsh. *Rachel.* A name like *Emily* flows too easily and is too soft. Stumbling instead of *going* or *headed* to the bathroom implies urgency. We have established now this is a man-woman scene. Alluding to the *War of 1812* accomplishes two things: there is an implication of violence or war, but it also controls pace, slowing it down to allow the reader to visualize the scene. The sentence would be ruined if you somehow tried to inform your reader (info-dump) that the War of 1812 refers to music. Unless you are writing to a young audience, your readers will instantly hear the percussion. Give your readers credit. This would be weakened and even a little insulting to the reader's intelligence if the sentence read: … *the War of 1812, Tchaikovsky's symphony replete with the sound of cannons.*

He fumbled for the key and thrust it into the lock.

Fumbling indicates he is not in control. Thrusting it into the lock could allude to sexual violence.

He heard the toilet flush, and twisted the key. "Dammit. Just open the door. I won't hurt you."

Turning the key has no emotional weight. *Twisting* the key is more aggressive and this is shaping up to be an aggressive story. You *turn* the pages of a book; you *twist* a knife in someone's back. By the way, this story is an example of a story created by a premise rather than a plot outline. I had no idea where this story would go. I still don't; I only had the premise of the prompt.

His saying *"I won't hurt you"* further indicates the potential for violence and the woman's anticipation of it.

Rachel jammed her legs into her jeans and slid her T-shirt over her bare shoulders. She tripped over her boots as she staggered to the window. For a moment, her father stopped beating on the door.

Ok. A direction for the story is given. It is not the police or a jealous lover or a landlord after rent or a pimp or a drug dealer. It's her father. The urgency is amplified, and we are getting clues for what may have happened. Why should I tell you what those possibilities are? Offer to let your readers speculate. I still have not decided myself what happened or will happen. I prefer to let Rachel tell you when she is ready. Jeans and T-shirt indicate the generation to which she belongs—no elegant or formal dress. Also, your choice of verbs getting her over to the window allows endless possibilities for you as a creative writer, as each verb has different implications: staggered/rushed/tiptoed/slinked/crawled/ bolted to/etc.

Once more he demanded entry, and once more he was refused. Once more he twisted the key, which conspired against him and broke off in the lock.

Here I am slowing down the action. A little foreplay is always appreciated! I am also giving human characteristics to an inanimate object, the key, personification. Add it as a tool in your work belt. Notice also *repetition* of a phrase as in a previous paragraph. "Thrice times I offered him a kingly crown which he did thrice times refuse." Here is another example of giving your writer credit. I am trusting you to recognize Marc Anthony's eulogy to Caesar. People who by choice will read your book will know this. Repetition of sounds or phrases can be very powerful and reinforcing.

Rachel could see Raul disappear down Kleine Mantelgasse under the
amber of a streetlamp. She closed the window and the room reverberated
like the inside of a drum, as a shoulder loaded with 120 kilos of rage
assaulted and splintered the door. He had to break through the door, as any
father would.

A prompt does not necessarily have to launch your story. Here it is actually split in two parts. It is important for all stories to quickly establish time and place. Rather than saying "this takes place on a ground floor apartment in Germany," we establish that for the reader by providing a German street name, and by Raul's escape—not likely if this was four flights up. (Refer to Lesson Five, the Info-dump.) We now know it is a ground-floor apartment and it is in the evening. Further proof that we're not in Kansas anymore is that we're talking kilos, not pounds. We are in Europe without saying we are in Europe. We are also allowing that the "villain" may have better motives than we originally thought, making him a complex character instead of a generic bad guy. Using the name *Raul* is intentional, because it sounds foreign in the context of the story being set in Germany, opening up the possibility or conflicts and tensions later in the story. "*Rachel* could see *Raul*" and "*under* the *amber*" and "*room reverberated*" are classic examples of how the lyrical nature of alliteration helps slide the words off the page and into your mind. (*lyrical*, paired with *alliteration*, is also alliteration.)

And why is she closing the window? Let your reader speculate.

So, now we are assuming that Rachel's lover had just made an escape. But are we sure? Maybe he was her drug dealer and she traded sex for drugs. Maybe it was a gay friend who came to visit while Rachel had been sleeping naked on the bed and Rachel fears her father's homophobia? Maybe they were planning a surprise birthday party for her father and didn't want him to find out? It's your show. Be absurd or conventional. Still endless possibilities. How would you finish this short scene?

We also get a partial description of the father. 120 kilos and strong. Use similes sparingly ... *reverberating like the inside of a drum.*

His daughter pressed her shoulders to the wall farthest away from him,
bracing herself. After a moment without a word passing between them, he
sat on the bed and began to rub his shoulder.

The potential for violence subsides. In the larger sense, if this were a novel, the approach to the door was the beginning, and breaking down the door was the climax. What happens now is a cooling off, a denouement.

> *She eased away from the wall and sat beside him. "You hurt yourself,"she said.*
> *"Yes."*
> *She kissed his cheek.*
> *"You hurt yourself," he said.*
> *She looked through the open door to the toilet before she answered.*
> *"Yes."*

So now the reader can infer that what was flushed down the toilet was probably not a condom or a pink pregnancy strip, but drugs. It is important not to reveal more than you have to so that the reader can be an active participant in your story and not just a passive witness.

Here is the full story, uninterrupted by comments:

"No. No fucking way."

"Just open the goddamn door."

Rachel gathered the evidence and stumbled to the bathroom to the beat of a man's heavy fist on a heavy door, pounding to the War of 1812.

He fumbled for the key and thrust it into the lock. He heard the toilet flush, and twisted the key. "Dammit. Just open the door. I won't hurt you."

Rachel jammed her legs into her jeans and slid her T-shirt over her bare shoulders. She tripped over her boots as she staggered to the window. For a moment, her father stopped beating on the door. Once more he demanded entry, and once more he was refused. Once more he twisted the key, which conspired against him and broke off in the lock.

Rachel could see Raul disappear down Kleine Mantelgasse under the amber of a streetlamp. She closed the window and the room reverberated like the inside of drum, as a shoulder loaded with 120 kilos of rage assaulted and splintered the door. He had to break through the door, as any father would.

His daughter pressed her shoulders to the wall farthest away from him, bracing herself. After a moment without a word passing between them, he sat on the bed and began to rub his shoulder.

She eased away from the wall and sat beside him. "You hurt yourself," she said.

"Yes."

She kissed his cheek.

"You hurt yourself," he said.

She looked through the open door to the toilet before she answered.

"Yes."

Hope this helps.

LESSON 11:

Your Turn

WORKOUT

Assignment: Here's your chance to use all the muscles you started training since A Prologue. Write one or two pages to this prompt: *Love Lost.*

Imagine that you have had a recent encounter with your first love. What do you say? What do you think? What do you feel? What has changed? And the most vexing question: *What if?* 500 to 750 words. Maybe that first love was the Ford Mustang, rediscovered in a used car lot when you came home one summer to see the folks. Maybe it was that rescue puppy from the pound, whose own soul was the reincarnation of the pup you got as a kid for Christmas. Maybe it was the woman you could never live without, or the man you could never live with.

Write swiftly. Set a timer for half an hour. This will keep you from over-thinking what you mean to say and be closer to the emotional truth of your story.

When you're done, and not before, go back and edit. See if you have absorbed the advice proffered so far about literary devices, info-dumps, adjectives. attribution, etc.

The next step is to do nothing.

After a day or two, come back to the story, but first re-read Harrington's laws of Novel Writing. Before you go in for another pass to edit, can you recall the first line of your story? If it does not immediately come to mind, you need a different first line. Victor Villaseñor has a litmus test by which he judges a writer's credibility: "Can they recall the first line to their novel?" Those who struggle to answer fail the test.

The wisdom of Horace Walpole still lingers after 250 years: "The world is a comedy to those who think, a tragedy to those who feel." Where is your story on this continuum?

———•———

If you've signed up for the Interactive Course, you know that submission for review of any eight assignments will garner you a Certificate of Completion. To reward exceptional efforts, if you successfully apply the bulk of the principles discussed in *Fire in the Belly* to this assignment, you'll be issued a Certificate of Excellence. Expect that the draft you send me will be returned with suggestions, much as I did for Juan Vandendorp until his submission reached its peak. Details of the Interactive Course are here:

https://gumroad.com/l/IPaVR

Good luck with this assignment.

LESSON 12:

Memorable Memoirs

The number is now six. I started keeping count after three.

That is the number of times over the years that the first words from someone, upon discovering I am a publisher and editor, is "I am not a writer, but …"and then the not-a-writer produces or informs me they have 300 pages of manuscript yellowing in the bottom drawer of their dresser or lurking behind their computer screen. You do not need the validation of an agent or publisher to genuinely assert that you are a writer, if you *write*. (By the way, the lead sentence, "I'm not a writer, but …" illustrates my point that injecting the word "but" undermines and contradicts the intent of the preceding clause.)

The boundaries between memoir and novel are often unguarded, whole stretches of border are void of uncoiled concertina wire, making it possible to drift from one territory to the other unabated, even, undetected. In a novel, you can masquerade as your protagonist and any or all of your peripheral characters and survive the scrutiny of immigration officers who compare your face to your passport photo, but if you're writing a memoir, you can't travel incognito.

Your purpose for writing a memoir may be somewhat more nuanced than for writing a novel, but, regardless of the genre, the same imperative applies to both endeavors: infuse your manuscript with conflict.

Your protagonist in a novel, or peripheral characters—hell, *every* character—could be a surrogate for you (as Milan Kundera points out)! If you're writing a novel, you are anticipating (at the risk of getting ahead of yourself) a general audience, and while this may also be true of a memoir, it's possible your target audience is confined to those you know and love, and is a desire to cement your legacy, either to distort or correct the perceptions this small readership may have of you. The chances are that you want to make sure your children and grandchildren remember not only who you are, but what is imperative for them to grasp in order to learn from your own experience navigating your life. Do you have questions that you regret never having asked your elders? Are they the same questions that someday your children may regret never having asked you? Answer before they ask. Committing yourself to documenting your life in the form of a memoir to them is like providing them with an instruction manual for life, that only you can author. It is the extreme act of love and caring.

To get started, if you haven't already done so, I suggest you pick one small incident that has stayed with you, rather than trying to make a map of all your time on the planet. You memorized dates in the fifth grade, only to discover as you matured that the dates spoke only of chronology, but nothing of history. When you graduated, when you got married/divorced, fell in love for the umpteenth time, when you moved to Philly; these are statistics, the listing of numbers in a phone book.

What about *you*? Your life is more than points on a graph.

Begin anywhere. Your first efforts amount to piano tuning. Pick something innocuous, such as going to the pound and picking out a puppy, or something horrendous, like receiving your draft notice or the discovery of cancer, or infidelity. You will be tempted to create your story as something linear, chronological, but as you begin writing, you'll quickly discover some episodes in your life carry more weight than others. Focus on these. Your children will want to know not only what you did with and in your life, but what you thought and felt along the way.

A memoir *need not* be directed exclusively towards your heirs, and though you might intend it for everyone held by gravity to the globe, I subscribe to the fairly-well accepted principle that when you write, write as if you are telling the story to just one person.

Recently I bellied up to a bar in Bohemia that smelled of Hemingway. The bartender, a somewhat evasive Honduran, confessed upon hearing I was a publisher that he kept a journal (after the gratuitous *I'm not a writer, but …*)

We bargained. An opinion on his first three pages in exchange for a rum and coke. I prepared myself, given the circumstances, to be underwhelmed. Instead, I discovered prose as beautiful as any I had ever encountered. The first of almost a thousand pages documenting an adventure and a truly impossible love story.

"What is this?" I asked, stupefied.

"It's about me and Emma. We walked across Africa together."

Not drove, not hitchhiked: *walked*.

He told me more, much more. Fraught with conflicts and obstacles, surviving horrific circumstances as in a novel, his was a love story that endured until it didn't, a casualty of the journey, but he could never forget her.

He poured me my payment. Usually, I stipulate that all fees are paid in advance, but as I was already running up a tab, I figured I had recourse if he didn't pay up.

"What do you want to see happen with this?"

"I want a book out of it."

"Of course." Isn't that what every writer tells me? But he continued.

"Just one book."

"Just one?"

"Yes. To give to Emma. So she will know I loved her."

Wow. A thousand pages of wow.

What finer motive can there be to writing your story than to present it to the ones you love to authenticate what you feel for them? Isn't your life a novel, really? Not an aimless meandering, but something with purpose and value? You are the central character, and you have faced with obstacles along the way. Did they beat you down? Did you overcome them? And most importantly, what did you learn that will help those who follow you to live fuller, more creative, productive, and satisfying lives? They can learn so much from your stories, but not if you don't tell them.

———————

Sometimes a dog just keeps scratching at the door until you let him out; sometimes a story is a pony in a corral before a rainstorm, feeling energized by the pending thunder and lightning, leaping the fence. And sometimes a writer is ten-months-big in a nine-month-womb. (Make sure you get your own story out before the shelf life expires, to insure freshness!) Urgency for a writer is inspiration on steroids.

I heard the pleadings and felt the urgency in Fred Rivera, a very humble man who several years ago approached me with a work-in-progress, a memoir of his time in Vietnam. The war left him drug and alcohol-addicted, poisoned by Agent Orange, crippled in body and spirit. Within a few pages of his rough draft, he shared this epiphany "Twenty-seven years after I got on the flight home, I saw that Nam war was just *raw man*, spelled backwards. I'm pretty raw today."

Though a memoir, I encouraged the author to structure the telling like a novel, making it more than a chronology of anecdotes. This he did with energy and talent.

Fred strapped himself into his chair as if it were the track he powered into battle a half-a-century ago, and bled out *Raw Man*, which won the Isabel Allende Best New Fiction award when we published it in 2015. Central to the story, Herman Johnson, a string-bean-of-a-kid from Detroit and Fred's best friend, dies in his arms.

But that's not the story I want to tell. You can find that at *www.rawman thebook.com*. Here's that happy ending I promised you in Lesson 4.

As Fred got sober and recovered from the laceration of body and spirit, he developed his capacity to help other vets suffering from PTSD and became a counselor, saving the lives of suicide-prone combat soldiers. One such soldier Fred rescued was Sgt. John Marek, an Afghan vet, who, in appreciation for what Fred had done for him, decided to get a pencil etching of Herman Johnson's name from the Vietnam Memorial Wall in D.C.

But he couldn't find the name. And then he had the most peculiar thought: what if Herman didn't die? Sgt. Marek was no stranger to the fog of war, and after intense research, he found someone matching Herman's particulars living in Detroit. He apprised Fred of the situation and asked if he should pursue the leads.

Fred, overwrought by the possibilities issued a flustered response: "Stand down."

Fred kept a letter in his breast pocket for two weeks, and then, on impulse, sent it to the address Sgt. Marek had provided.

Three days later, Fred got the phone call ….

"Fred?"

"Herman?"

Each thought the other had died.

A Word with You Press organized a GoFundMe campaign to reunite the two in the obvious location: The Vietnam Memorial Wall in our nation's capital.

Herman, who had been severely wounded in the battle Fred recreates in

Reunited by the magic of the written word. Welcome home.
© Thornton Sully

Raw Man, woke up in a field morgue to find his dog-tag between his teeth, the army equivalent of a yellow tag on the big toe. Yet, for obfuscated reasons, Herman was never awarded a Purple Heart.

Unbeknownst to Herman, Fred worked tirelessly behind the

scenes before their reunion, enlisting the aid of General Guy Swan, himself a Vietnam vet, to be on hand to preside over the event.

"Sergeant: Read the orders."

A crisply uniformed Sgt. John Marek marched forward, and pivoted to address the curious, growing audience, with Fred and Herman standing at attention to the side of the general.

"By order of the President of the United States, for wounds sustained in combat in Vietnam in 1969, the Purple Heart is hereby awarded Private First- Class Herman Johnson."

Applause, spontaneous, and not a dry eye. I still get teary-eyed thinking about it.

"Welcome home, son. It took us 47 years to right this wrong." After a salute, General Swan swept Herman, still bewildered by what had just occurred, into his arms.

And now my point: None of this would have happened if Fred had not locked himself into his computer and told his story.

You will never know the effects of telling your story, until you tell it.

———————

If you're still too shy to ask your muse for a date, let me tell you about my friend, Victor Villaseñor, the prolific best-selling author of *Rain of Gold*, the story of his family settling in Oceanside, California, after being driven north to escape the calamity unleashed by a decade of the Mexican Revolution in 1910.

Victor was an admittedly angry 20-year-old, having endured not only racist taunts and attitudes in the local school, but also having suffered humiliation administered openly by his teachers, who did not recognize that Victor was dyslexic, and felt no restraint to broadcast their judgment of him to his classmates that he was, simply, stupid.

So, one bright California afternoon, Victor loaded up his pickup truck with guns and bullets, drove from the formidable hacienda his father had established, and headed north, intent on violence. The opportunity came in Wyoming. As Victor tells it, from the road he could see a herd of elk grazing on a plateau, and his adrenaline started pumping. He strapped on his pistol, and un-swaddled the rifle riding shotgun beside him. He slipped down a shallow canyon, unseen by the herd, with the plan to traverse the escarpment downwind, and take aim at the buck farthest away. When the buck dropped, he reasoned, the herd would stampede in the opposite direction, straight towards himself, and he could then shoot as many of them as he had bullets in his pistol as they panicked past him. Easy money.

Having scaled the ravine, he crept forward, rifle to his chest. He lay prone, and planted the stock to his shoulder, but standing in his way to a clear shot of the buck was a doe, and her two fawns, grazing lazily with their tails twitching towards the determined assassin. The doe heard or sensed Victor's presence, and, rather than skittering away, turned, and started ambling endearingly in his direction, her fawns in tow. She paused and stared directly into Victor's eyes, and in that moment of her gaze, was transformed into a Yaqui Indian woman, reminiscent to Victor of his grandmother, the woman who seeded his imagination with the myths and folklore of her tribe, stories that would form the foundation of his later works.

Victor tried to rub the illusion from his eyes, literally, but could not, as the woman stood passively before him, unperturbed by the malice in his heart and his intention to slaughter. The vision of the Yaqui woman was no mirage and would not evaporate. In her calming presence, Victor relaxed his chokehold on his rifle, and had this cathartic epiphany. "I knew at that moment," he told me, "I really didn't want to kill any living thing. I wanted to kill the rage in my heart."

As the moment unfolded, on that expansive plateau in Wyoming, Victor, whose life until then was without known purpose, struck up a bargain with God. "God, make me a writer. If you do, I promise to write the untold stories of my people."

God was amused, but not dismissive. "Victor, all right, but we have a problem. You're illiterate."

Victor thought it over. "OK. I'll learn how to read and write."

God acquiesced.

Back at his family home in Oceanside, Victor made good on his part of the bargain. Every day for six months, to overcome his dyslexia, he trained himself by writing the text of the same page over and over again with paper and pencil (still his preferred method of composing) until he could do it fluidly.

Apparently, God held up his end of the bargain as well. Victor's body of work, beginning with *Macho* and best-selling *Rain of Gold*, *Burro Genius*, *Thirteen Senses* and so on, is extensive, and critics compare him to John Steinbeck. In recent years, like Steinbeck, Victor has been nominated for a Pulitzer Prize. Still might get it.

Here is a final concept for this first volume of lessons and insights I want to share with you: *bookending*. It's metaphoric meaning can be divined by the word itself. Imagine your books on a shelf, sandwiched on the left and right with a bookend, consolidating everything in between. A literary example might be starting a story with:

> *It's going to be a good day,* thought Arianna. She led Bubba, the roan, out of the stall, just as the morning sun was prodding the clouds, still asleep on the hillside and not fully aware that the day had begun ....

***

... A lot of stuff (i.e., your novel) happens. The *bookending* would be something like this:

> The clouds, exhausted by their labors of the day shading the farm, clocked out and nestled to sleep on the soft hillside, just as the moon lit the way for Arianna to lead Bubba back to his stall. Though things had not gone exactly according to plan, Arianna had cause to be pleased with herself. It had been a good day, after all.

The bookend for *Fire in the Belly: How to write your novel with Purpose and Passion?* I asked as you began these lessons to clearly articulate *why* you write, or want to write, and now we bookend with the confirmation that the Honduran, Fred, and Victor *all* knew the *why* before even considering the *what*. The *why* for that bartender in Bohemia was to tell Emma he loved her. The *why* for the Vietnam veteran was to expose the horror and consequences of combat, an impassioned protest against ill-conceived wars, and the *why* for the reluctant rifleman was to give voice to the voiceless, sparing them of the kind of anguish he himself faced as a denigrated illiterate. Only when these three had answered why they write, were they able to know *what* to write.

Your job as the author is to cover the *why* and *what*. My job, the job of every editor, is to help you with the *how*. What an editor wants from you above all else is the story inhabiting your manuscript. Everything else—style, rhetoric, rhythm, story arc, character and plot development—is malleable.

So … we've addressed the questions of *Why, What,* and *How*. All that's left is *When*. **Why not now?**

LESSON 12:

Memorable Memoirs

WORKOUT

"In order to write about life first you must live it."

Ernest Hemingway

Assignment: Hemingway lived an extraordinary, adventurous life, not more so than a multitude of others, but what truly distinguished him from them was that he wrote about it. Maybe you never ran the bulls in Pamplona, used your skull as a battering ram to escape a burning plane on a remote airstrip in Africa or smuggled arms into Cuba or Spain. That does not disqualify you from writing an extraordinary novel or memoir.

> "You do not need to leave your room. Remain sitting at your table and listen. Do not even listen, simply wait, be quite still and solitary. The world will freely offer itself to you to be unmasked, it has no choice, it will roll in ecstasy at your feet."

Franz Kafka

Paraphrasing Nietzsche, behind every great artist is an ordinary man, and behind every ordinary man is a great artist. You've occupied a unique space on the planet. Tell us about it. Write the first page of your novel as if it is a memoir, *or* write the first page of your memoir as if it is a novel.

Before We Say Goodbye

You may know this story.

The waters along the shore had retreated excessively during a spring tide, stranding thousands of starfish left dehydrating on the beach as far as the eye could see. An old man on his morning stroll watched as a young girl was frantically tossing as *many* of them as she could as *far* as she could, back into the ocean. The old man looked up and down the beach at the infinite

© Pexels/Pixabay

number of starfish in each direction, and scoffed, "Do you really think it will make any difference?"

"Yes. To the ones I toss back in the sea."

Your story—what you have to offer, what you have to say—may not find its way to the New York Times best-seller list, but it may very well find the select audience that will be enchanted and inspired by your words, and grateful you made the effort to write them. Your work could keep someone from dehydrating, and could add meaning to their lives.

We are all conformists, but the difference among people is whether it is to their *fears* or their *desires* that they conform. Conform to your fear that you're not good enough? Or conform to your desire to be an exceptional writer, well-respected for your ability to convey your stories with passion, clarity and purpose—in other words, with eloquence.

I'm listening. Ready *when* you are! And one final bit of advice:

Tell your muse you think she's hot!

Here's wishing you fire in the belly!
Czeers!
Thorn Sully,
Editor-in-Chief
A Word with you Press

TESTIMONIALS

I toiled long and hard for years on my book *Raw Man* before I met Thornton Sully. He helped me realize that I did have a story to tell and his belief in me raised my own hopes of being a published author. I would never have had such a wonderful experience without his enthusiastic help. He is easy to work with and a joy to be around. He guided me through the rough spots and, as a team, we created a work that has drawn praise.

Fred Rivera
Winner *2015 Isabel Allende Miraposa Award*
for Best New Fiction 2015

I have known Thorn in friendship over the past 15 years ... However, I was not really aware of his superb talent for editing and developmental assistance. Over the last five years, I worked on my manuscript ... a self-help project with a new twist for helping readers to heal their interpersonal relationship matters. Although I had previously written a children's program for self-empowerment versus relational aggression, soon and produced a character-building card deck, this new manuscript was a hefty project. Luckily, Thorn came to my rescue.

Rather than agonizing over the next collaborative editing session, I actually found myself looking forward to our meetings and Thorn's refined tutelage. Thorn intuitively seemed to get where I was going and lent remarkably sound and salient advice for honing and refining my manuscript to its best outcome. Thorn has great "people skills" and is able to impart his professional wisdom including constructive critiques in a very firm yet gentle and palliative way. I emerged from Thorn's care with a new-found confidence regarding my recently published manuscript. I have already sung his praise to many of my friends and colleagues. I highly encourage you to allow Thorn to take the helm and steer your writings past any stormy seas and into a safe harbor ... where the sun shines brightly, and you can wiggle your toes in the warm sand ... knowing you have arrived!

Kristine Grant
Licensed Marriage and Family Therapist
Relationshift © How to write the words you really want to say

The funny thing about working with Thorn is that I can't exactly say what he does that helps me. I usually start out not agreeing with his suggestions, only to end up following them. Maybe it's the very act of resisting his ideas that serves as an exercise in clarification. After all, more times than not, this exercise leads me to see the wisdom of his direction. Perhaps it's Thorn's practical wisdom on the art and craft of writing. I'm still not sure. All I know is I've become a better writer since working with Thorn.

Mark Cohen
Attorney at Law

Thornton Sully is one of the best editors I've ever worked with. Several years ago I wrote a memoir that needed editing. Before I met Thorn, I retained a well-respected and highly recommended editor to red line my manuscript. It took her several months and the results were helpful, but not what I was looking for. So, when Thorn brought up the idea of sending the first few pages of my manuscript to him to review for free, I was hopeful, but didn't expect much. I'm so glad I sent them over. I learned more in two pages from him than I did on the entire manuscript from the other editor! I quickly retained his services to help me with the rest of my book. The quality jumped up markedly. Another thing I appreciate is Thorn's interactions. Some editors are too harsh; others are pushovers. Thorn has the perfect balance of respecting your feelings and artistic choices, while strongly voicing his opinion (which usually makes the book much better). I didn't always agree with everything he said, but the way he said it never got my back up, which is an art in itself.

Since retaining his services for my book, I have also invited him to contribute to *Legacy Arts*, which is a magazine my company publishes. It's the leading publication for *Meaning Legacy planning* and is distributed to financial professionals, business executives, and philanthropists all over the United States. He's able to quickly get the gist of an idea without much direction and write something of exceptional quality. My company (Paragon Road) also works with people who want to write their own life stories either as an exercise in self-exploration or to pass on to their families and I have recommended his services to them as a writing coach and creative editor.

Laura Roser
CEO and Editor-in-Chief
Legacy Arts Magazine

I have had the pleasure of working with Thornton Sully now for the past few years. He recently worked on an historical fiction novel for my client. He is exceptionally talented as a developmental editor/ghost writer. He reworked an already great manuscript by smoothing out the rough spots; putting action into areas where there was too much dialogue; adding dialogue into areas where there was too much story; fleshing out characters; adding details that pull the reader into the story further; weeding out extraneous or repetitive text; building greater drama; possessing a keen eye for details; while being ever aware of the author's voice and feelings. His suggestions were excellent. His references were vast and excellent. I have met many of the people he has done work for and ALL sing his praise. I am sincerely honest with all that I have said about Thorn, and you would be most fortunate to have him bless your story. Thorn is a classy, extremely intelligent gentleman who I am proud to know and work with. I will be definitely utilizing his great gifts on future projects.

Jan Kalish
Publishing Project Manager

Thorn and I worked in collaboration for Mo Bjornestad, the founder of the SafeTFirst Corporation, who developed an innovative range of personal safety and tracking apps that interface with Emergency Services and other First Responders.

We held conference calls with the client, agreed to a schedule of work, created web and product content, and also drafted promotional scripts. Our primary objective was to assimilate technical details and then make that information reader-friendly and engaging. Our client, Mo, was happy to sign-off on our work.

Derek Thompson
Author, Thomas Bladen *detective series*

Since I write tons of offers, articles, and book parts every year, I have often been utilizing various editing services often. As you might have guessed, it hasn't been the easiest journey. On top of the fact that most of my writing is voluntary, I had to spend a lot of money and time to deal with editing and publishing.

So what are my conclusions?

First, there are editors and there are Editors. My current editor, Thornton Sully, is an example of the latter. He is a strategic editor, who supports you not only with the writing itself but also the whole strategy and tactics, so your book/article has a much better chance of being accepted by publishers. When you need to improve the structure of your piece or its appeal, he's right there. When you are struggling with grammar or syntax, he's also there. When your inspiration runs out, he will even do some writing for you.

Most importantly, Thorn is a person I could talk (yes, TALK) to and share my doubts and ideas. My mind clears of writing clutter and my heart engages in my writing because he understands my aims and motivations. If you need a mixture of a writing mentor and coach with a good dose of empathetic prodding, this is a great address.

So, start here, with an Editor. Your writing and your soul will not regret Thorn's strategic and supportive approach.

Jacek 'Skyski' Skrzypczynski
executive coach & MBA professor,
author of the bestselling book series:
Discover Your Undefeated Spirit

EDITING AND PUBLISHING SERVICES AND FEES

Your story, *your* truth, is important to me, and I never lose sight of the fact that you are the world's leading authority on your own work. So how do I help you? I do so by investing heart and mind into your project, as you have done.

My editing fees are as follows:

First 30 pages review:	no charge
Manuscript overview:	$2 per page
One 20-hour block of time:	$1,200*
*Quick edit or consultation:	$85 per hour

Reading and commenting on your first 30 pages without assessing a fee is not altruistic; it gives me an opportunity to demonstrate how I can help you, and why you need me. There have been only a few instances when a working author/editor relationship did not follow the *pro bono* assessment. Send your first 30 pages, double spaced Times New Roman 12-point font as a word doc attachment to me at thorn@awordwithyoupress.com, and in the subject line indicate "*Pro Bono* Assessment." I'll return it to you with *specific* recommendations in the format of track changes, with my reasoning behind each suggestion.

Included in the $2-per-page overview are specific recommendations documented as track changes for your first 30 pages, plus my professional opinion of the manuscript as a whole. Will people keep turning pages? If not, then why? How can we change that? After an evaluation of your strengths and weaknesses, I'll provide a strategic blueprint to guide you through edits and rewrites to bring your work to its fullest potential.

Your second block of time (20 hours) is also $1,200. Subsequent blocks of time are discounted to $1,000. Only in rare instances do we require more than two blocks of time, and generally, with give-and-take correspondence, you and I will need about six weeks to get the full value of our first 20 hours working together.

---

* If you opt for the overview first, I deduct half of what you have paid up to $300 for your first block of time. For example, if you have paid me $420 to read a 210-page manuscript, your first block of time would be $990).

Though my passion is for memoir and literary fiction, I also have assisted authors of non-fiction, self-help, and young adult books, mainstream fiction, romance, sci-fi and so on. Don't hesitate to tell me about your project in any genre, and your publishing aspirations: thorn@awordwithyoupress.com

PROOOOFREADING

While I catch many errors in grammar, syntax, noun-verb and tense agreement and spelling, typos, etc., my focus is on the broader issues of story arc, plot, character development and style. So, I do not warrant that I will catch all the proofreading errors, and I defer that to others on my team at a rate of $2 per page. Generally, at *A Word with You Press*, we adhere to the Chicago Manual of Style.

We'll go through the process together, and the day will come when you realize you're done and ready to pop the champagne. All dressed up and nowhere to go?

Let's get you up and out the door.

PUBLISH WITH US

A Word with You Press has published over 30 books since 2009, and we'd be happy to consider your work to add to the list. You are free to engage your own editors, but we reserve the right to decline publishing work that fails professional and ethical standards.

We have 25 years' experience. In addition to having edited and published a stable of repeat clients, we are contracted to provide design services for the International Federation of Red Cross Red Crescent Societies, the Climate Center, the Netherlands Red Cross, the Belgian Red Cross, the International Institute for Environment and Development and the Library of the Hungarian Academy of Sciences, demanding organizations requiring exacting results. In addition, we have published award-winning writers, and have helped utterly unknown writers become recognized award-winners.

For a comprehensive exploration of publishing with *A Word with You Press*, send us an email and a brief explanation of your project, and we'll respond with an invitation to schedule a Skype or Zoom call, or some similar venue.

What's your story?

A Word with You Press

Editors and Advocates for Fine Stories in the Digital Age

with offices and affiliates in the USA, the UK, Germany, Poland, and the Czech Republic

www.awordwithyoupress.com

A WORD ABOUT

A Word with You Press
Editors and Advocates of Fine Stories in the Digital Age

A Word with You Press is a playful, passionate, and prolific consortium of writers, editors, designers and publishers who have been helping authors like yourself achieve their goals since 2009. We are drawn to the notion that nothing is more beautiful or powerful than a story well told. We help you tell it.

Writers and artists don't just happen; they are created by nurturing, mentoring, and by damn good editing. We provide this literary triad through our interactive website, www.awordwithyoupress.com. Our regular writing contests grant you the opportunity to hone your skills, and receive both professional and peer feedback, as your entries are published on the site and invite commentary.

We have helped first-time authors become award winners, and we, ourselves, have won awards for writing, editing, and publishing excellence. The first step to writing your novel? Intent. If you've got it, let's talk. Send inquiries to thorn@awordwithyoupress.com

 Thornton Sully has Jack-Londoned his way across the globe sleeping with whatever country would have him and picking up stray stories along the way. A litter of dog-eared passports, seaman's papers and visas that have taken up residence in his sock drawer are a constant temptation, but, as the founder in 2009 of this literary enterprise, dedicated to helping you write and publish your story persuasively and with passion, it's not likely he will stray too far from the towers that are *A Word with You Press*, now located in the Bohemian metropolis Ceske Budejovice in the Czech Republic, except, perhaps, for an occasional swim in the Aegean. Authors who have sought his advice have won major awards, including the Pulitzer Prize, the Isabel Allende Miraposa Award for new fiction, and the Best Poetry Award from San Diego Writers' Awards.

"I arise in the morning torn between a desire to improve the world and a desire to enjoy the world. This makes it hard to plan the day."

Thornton Sully,
plagiarizing E.B. White

Made in the USA
Middletown, DE
10 November 2021